*My Way* is Vol. 2 of the Wakestone Legacy Series.

The Wakestone Legacy Series is about approachable history. Stories of the people who shaped our nation and culture and upon whose shoulders we all stand. Written for young adults (of all ages), these books bring alive the men and women we know we are supposed to know.

We are the beneficiaries of the experiences of those who came before, but their stories have too often been lost amongst the press of scholarship, buried under the need for the new and controversial. The Wakestone Legacy Series biographies bring their stories into a modern context and allow us to see them through a new, brighter lens.

Elvis Presley had a vision of who he wanted to be, and it was different! *My Way* tells the story of how Elvis persevered and lived his dream to become an American idol in music and movies. Though he never wrote a song, he changed the music we listen to. With his inimitable style, his unique voice, his irrepressible charm, and his endearing touch of naïveté, Elvis paved the way for rock and roll to become the music of America and the world. Long after his death, Elvis is alive to new generations of fans who visit his home, Graceland, buy his records, and watch his films.

From a virtual overnight sensation in 1954 to the king of music in three years, Elvis grabbed our attention with his voice and his "erotic" gyrations. He galvanized and polarized the world to become the heartthrob of millions of girls and a demon to thousands of pulpits.

From his startling and controversial beginning, Elvis became the model for how to build and market a star, with his management team launching the first multimedia campaigns, broad merchandising deals, and stadium concerts. He was the original idol.

Yet beneath this idol was a gentle young man, constantly looking for love and acceptance, and the story of how he lived and died "his way" touches us deeply.

# MY WAY

## How Elvis Presley became ELVIS!

By Sherry Lee Hoppe

## Wakestone Legacy Series
## Volume 2

Wakestone Press
Nashville, Tennessee

My Way
How Elvis Presley became ELVIS!
By Sherry Lee Hoppe

Wakestone Legacy Series
Volume 2

Wakestone Press, L.L.C.
200 Brook Hollow Road
Nashville, TN 37205

http://www.wakestonepress.com

ISBN 13            ............................... 978-1-60956-013-3
ISBN 10            ........................................1-60956-013-2
Library of Congress Control Number.................2011945798

Cover design by Cathy Riviere
Edited by Frank Daniels III

Printed in the United States of America.

Titles in the Wakestone Legacy Series

**First Friend**
Thomas Jefferson: The original social networker.

**My Way**
How Elvis Presley became ELVIS!

# Table of Contents

# INTRODUCTION

*For what is a man, what has he got?*

*If not himself, then he has naught...*

~Paul Anka

If *American Idol* had been around in 1953 during mid to late summer and had stopped in Memphis to spot Tennessee talent, young Elvis Presley might have tried his luck on the *Idol* stage instead of paying $3.95 (about $32 in 2011) for his first acetate to be cut at Memphis Recording Services. More than five decades later, one wonders how *Idol* judges Randy Jackson, Stephen Tyler, and Jennifer Lopez would have critiqued Elvis the Pelvis.

Would Randy have rolled his eyes at the shy boy whose insecurity saturated his stage presence? Would he have asked, as Marion Keisker of Sun Records did, "What kind of singer are you?" and derided Elvis' response, "I sing all kinds." Would Randy have ruthlessly torn into the kid when Elvis answered his next question, "Who do you sound like?" and heard Elvis' reply, "I don't sound like nobody." Would he have declared, as entertainer Eddie Bond did in 1953, "...you're never going make it as a singer?" Or would Randy have seen beyond the jagged nasality, appreciating the fullness of tone? Would he have recognized the potential for that voice to electrify audiences, to run the gamut of genres? Would he have detected the multiple musical influences lurking in the shadow of the quavering notes?

Would Jennifer have danced with Elvis from her judge's chair, or would she have ridiculed the sensual gyrations of Elvis' left leg as it nervously jiggled in time to the music? Would she have been bemused by the way he cradled his beat-up, child-size guitar? Would she have detected the power he would someday hold over an audience and voted to give him a chance to demonstrate he could go from gospel to rhythm and blues (R&B) to country to rock 'n' roll?

And Stephen, would he have seen Elvis as fresh and exuberant, or would he have heard the plaintive crooning of "My Happiness" as an inept replay of an old tune? Would he have seen Elvis as a white man trying to sound black?

Would the *American Idol* audience have laughed at the kid with greasy hair and outlandish clothes, or would they have instinctively embraced Elvis as the symbol of their restlessness, their unspoken quest for music they could call their own? Would he have turned them off or transfixed them?

Like Sam Phillips (the man who recorded Elvis' first record), the *American Idol* judges might have initially missed *why* Elvis didn't sound like anyone else—described by Barker and Taylor as "two completely distinct approaches to the upper and lower registers: a baritone quaver that sounded like someone was pounding him on the chest and a tenor so pure it was ghostly." It was all there that day when Elvis strode sheepishly into the recording studio, saying he wanted to cut a record for his mother's birthday (which had actually occurred a few months earlier). Fortunately, Marion saw what Sam missed, and eventually she persuaded him to give Elvis a chance. The rest is history, an American dream come true—from rags to riches, from rural obscurity to international fame.

Ignoring callous criticism and attempts to establish him as the root of generational evil, Elvis did it *his* way and became *the* American idol. Although he never wrote a song, he made others' songs his own, becoming an icon whose unique brand of music has touched and charmed fans for more than 50 years. Long past his untimely death, he still sells records, attracts new fans, and endures in garnering the highest moneymaking status of all celebrities. In short, he has stayed famous— most likely because he dared to do it *his* way, refusing to stay inside one genre, rebelling against those who tried to subdue him, and responding vicariously to his audiences.

Elvis, his managers, business partners, and fans laid the foundation for an iconic brand that transcended media, and long after his death continues to be the standard against which entertainment fortunes are measured. The evolution of Elvis' legendary style holds the key to his prolonged popularity, with a wide range and variety of influences contributing to this style and his persona, uniquely connecting him to his people:

- A fascination with black gospel music and "negro field jazz" (described by one photo caption as a "white man's voice singing negro rhythms with a rural flavor")
- An accidental progression into the "rockabilly" style that melded rhythm/blues and country, blurring genre lines
- The intuitive recognition that teenagers were searching for a way to express their identity and the accompanying launch of rock 'n' roll, the genre that captured the imagination of this group that would later become known as the baby boom generation
- An insatiable quest to improve
- The development of a distinctive delivery based on an incredible instinct and innate ability to read his audience and adjust his performance to its response
- The capacity to take others' music and re-style it with his intensity and delivery
- The ability to use his quavering vibrato and natural falsetto range to communicate emotions that electrified listeners
- A fondness for flashy clothes and uninhibited movements (one writer calls them "weird wiggles") that set him apart from other singers
- A lifelong ambition to embrace and sing a diverse collection of music—country and western, gospel, ballads, R&B, even a near-operatic style and a "behind closed doors" interest in classical music.

In the end, all of these elements came together to create Elvis' idiosyncratic style, defying ongoing criticism by both music reviewers and self-proclaimed protectors of morality. Though Elvis' life was cut short, his music lives on—proof not only that he was a legitimate singer but also arguably the most original and continually evolving musical star of his era. Leonard Bernstein proclaimed him as "the greatest cultural force in the twentieth century." Even in life, he was a legend. But it was more than his singing that stirred hearts. His grace and his generosity, his loneliness and his rambunctiousness, and his foibles and his search for spiritual peace comprised a full, if sometimes conflicted, life. "But," biographer Pamela Clarke Keogh notes, "it is his humanity—not his perfection—that draws us to him, even today."

"My way" was Elvis' mantra and his cross.

# 1
# IN THE GHETTO

*On a cold and gray [Tupelo] morn*

*A poor little baby child is born.*

~Mac Davis

The East Tupelo shotgun house Vernon Presley built in anticipation of the birth of his first child didn't offer much protection from the cold, wind-swept weather in the winter of 1935. Still, it wasn't the ghetto, and in the middle of the Great Depression, it was more than many people had. Vernon and his wife Gladys were grateful to have a place to call their own.

In the two-room, unpainted shack, which sported a pump and an outhouse at the back, with the help of a midwife and a 68-year-old doctor Elvis Aron Presley emerged in a room lit by gas lanterns around 4:30 a.m. on January 8, 1935. Gladys cried, but it wasn't feeding a hungry mouth that troubled her—her tears stemmed from the stillborn birth of Elvis' twin, Jesse Garon. She hadn't even known she was carrying two babies—how could she? Like other poor people, she couldn't afford prenatal care. And when she finally arrived at the hospital after giving birth, she found she could never have any more children. Elvis was to be her only child. And his mama cried.

The three Presleys had a hard life in the poorest part of town, but the family never lacked love. Some say Gladys loved Elvis excessively— that she kept him *too* close to her, fearing the loss of her only son. But no one can question the bond the two shared. Unusually close to his mother, Elvis' emotional attachment to his father was also unmistakable. Like Gladys, Vernon constantly worried about something happening to Elvis, so the parents were prone not to let Elvis out of their sight in his early years, leading to an insular family—a tendency for isolation that would follow Elvis into his days of fame.

Although Vernon had no stocks and no money in a bank, he felt the long-term impact of the crash of America's economy along with everyone else. Jobs were scarce, and they never lasted long. The struggling father managed to feed his family through a series of odd jobs, including work as a milkman, a day laborer, a sharecropper, and a WPA carpenter. Some say he lacked ambition, but others believe he was merely the product of a hopeless time. Gladys helped out by working at the Tupelo Garment Factory, earning two dollars a day for a twelve-hour shift, until just before Elvis was born. It was a hard life, but it was good.

Although Elvis and his family, in Vernon's words, "formed [their] own private world," church and extended family played a part in Elvis' early years. Music in the Assembly of God, a "holy roller" church, held a strong attraction for the young boy, who joined in with fervor long before he knew the words to the songs. Gladys was fond of telling how, "when Elvis was just a little fellow, not more than two years old, he would slide down off my lap, run into the aisle and scramble up to the platform. There he would stand looking at the choir and trying to sing with them." He might not know the words, but he could carry the tune. And he loved the sounds of the musical instruments—brass, winds, banjos, drums, and guitars—which the Assembly used long before other Protestant churches moved beyond pianos and organs. So from an early age, Elvis was exposed to "making a joyful noise to the Lord" in a loud and vociferous way. It was music that made the little boy want to dance—or at least shake a leg and wave an arm.

The loving, if impoverished, life of the Presleys took a nosedive shortly after Elvis' debut with the church choir. Vernon, along with his brother Travis and another fellow, forged and cashed a four-dollar check, landing them all on a chain gang prison farm. A hard life got even harder. Unable to make payments on the shotgun house in Vernon's absence, Gladys and Elvis had to move in with family, even though Gladys took a job at the Mid-South Laundry. Being apart was tough, and most weekends Gladys and Elvis scraped up enough money for the bus fare required for the 10-hour round-trip to visit Vernon. Although Vernon was paroled eight months into his three-year sentence, the family's tenuous security had been shattered, and it would be years before the family would own a house again. Their world became one of temporary jobs and transitory housing.

# MY WAY

In his childhood, three constants composed Elvis' life—love, music, and poverty. Two were positives and one an endless worry. All would have a lasting impact, shaping who Elvis was and who he would become. The family never went hungry, Vernon declared, but he admitted some nights all they had for supper was cornbread and water. And music, a welcome diversion, waxed free on the radio, at church, and at outdoor concerts in Tupelo's Courthouse Square, so they never lacked for entertainment—even if they didn't have iPods or MP3 players.

Music drew Elvis like a magnet, an outlet for emotions he couldn't express and a source of peace in a life of uncertainty. Nonetheless, many were taken aback when the shy, tow-headed boy stood, at the age of ten, and sang "Old Shep" without accompaniment in front of an audience of several hundred at the Mississippi-Alabama Fair and Dairy Show. As the story goes, a neighbor had been impressed by Elvis' singing and brought him to the attention of his grade-school principal, who entered the ten-year-old in the fair's talent show. Various accounts of the day report that Elvis won second place, although Tupelo residents who attended the fair have disputed this. Elvis, so short he couldn't reach the microphone and had to stand on a chair, once said he thought he placed fifth. He was certain about one thing, though. His mother gave him a "whipping" that day for going on one of the fair's rides.

For his eleventh birthday, Elvis wanted a bicycle, but in the aftermath of World War II, money was tight and he got a guitar instead. In retrospect, some wonder if the guitar resulted from a shortage of money or from Gladys' ongoing burden, causing dread that Elvis might get run over by a car or have some other accident. Regardless, everyone agreed the guitar might help Elvis with his singing, and he was soon learning chords and runs from Frank Smith, the pastor of his church. A short time later, he began playing and singing at the Assembly.

During this time, Elvis also became a fan of local country-western singer Mississippi Slim. With a twang in his voice and a catch in his throat, Slim was pure country. Occasionally, he took young Elvis under his wing, teaching him more chords on his guitar and regaling him with tales of life on the road. Some think Slim let Elvis play before a live audience once or twice as part of WELO's Jamboree, a weekly amateur hour. Regardless, Slim undoubtedly helped Elvis form a solid alliance

# IN THE GHETTO

with hillbilly music. Singin' and pickin' became his passion.

In his *Up Close* book on Elvis, biographer Wilborn Hampton says, "Like Mary and her little lamb in the nursery rhyme, everywhere that Elvis went the guitar was sure to go." He even took it to school every day, except when it rained, pulling it from his locker at lunch to practice, especially after his family moved from East Tupelo into the "real" Tupelo, where they were viewed as poor white trash, a put-down that haunted Vernon. He was still talking about it not long before his death many years later: "Poor we were, I'll never deny that. But trash we weren't ....We never had any prejudice. We never put anybody down. Neither did Elvis."

In a new school, Elvis felt isolated, an outsider, likely because he lived in a racially segregated neighborhood and often wore overalls to school. Shake Rag, where the family rented its latest home, was packed with black churches and black schools. Elvis was forbidden by law to attend the neighborhood school since he was white, so he had to walk to another part of town to an all-white school. But on nights and weekends, black music wafted through the family's windows, propped open to catch a breeze on steamy summer nights. The blues, spirituals, and jazz sweeping the streets in close proximity to his bedroom spoke to Elvis' soul. He might have been on the outside, but inside he absorbed the black rhythm and plaintive voices until he felt one with them.

Mostly, Elvis kept his interest in music to himself, but he was dumbfounded when he made a "C" in music in the eighth grade. Incensed at the injustice, Elvis demanded to know why his music teacher didn't think he could sing. By golly, he *could* sing, and he would show her. The next day he lugged his little guitar to class and sang, "Keep Them Cold Icy Fingers Off of Me." The teacher reluctantly agreed Elvis could sing but hastily added she didn't appreciate his kind of singing. It wasn't the last time someone would denigrate his style and choice of music.

Or pick on him. One day, just after the beginning of the eighth grade, some of the school's bullies, who derided the white kid who lived in the "colored" section of town, decided to let Elvis know what they thought of him and his country music. Before Elvis realized what they were doing, they had grabbed his guitar and cut all of its strings. It was like seeing his fingers whacked off. But not all his classmates were so mean; seeing Elvis' misery at the bullying, his friends pooled their money and bought him a new set of strings. It was a kindness Elvis never forgot.

Whether that incident or Vernon's ongoing difficulty finding work was the final straw, it was not long thereafter that the Presleys packed their meager belongings in boxes, loaded them in the trunk and on top of their 1937 Plymouth, and headed to Memphis, about fifty miles north of Tupelo. Maybe there, in the big city, Vernon could find a steady job. It was 1949, and the war had been over for several years, but the Presleys were still moving every time the rent came due. And they were tired of it. Later, Elvis would say, "We were broke, man, broke. We left Tupelo overnight...and headed to Memphis. Things had to be better."

A fellow classmate remembers Elvis singing a few songs for his friends before he left, ending with "A Leaf on a Tree." The friend told Elvis, "You're going to be famous someday," and with a shy smile, Elvis responded, "I sure hope so."

# 2
# IF I CAN DREAM

*If I can dream of a better land. . .*

*Tell me why, oh why, oh why can't my dream come true?*

~Walter Earl Brown

Because of its unique location on a high bluff on the Mississippi River, Memphis flourished as a trade center hosting large markets in agriculture and natural resources well into the 20th century. When the Presley family arrived in Memphis, it was the world's largest market for cotton and hardwood lumber. It was also the home of the first self-service grocery store and the first supermarket chain, Piggly Wiggly. As commercial Memphis embraced change, it also clung to its past, as home to the largest mule market in the world.

The mixture of old and new was reflected in Memphis' unique brand of Southern politics as well. For almost four decades beginning in the 1910s, it was a hotbed of machine politics under the tutelage of E. H. "Boss" Crump. White folk knew the real reason Crump allowed blacks to vote and whispered about how he manipulated their vote with fear; but as long as he controlled the "coloreds," that was okay with them.

Memphis only seemed racially progressive—"polite" society mirrored the behavior of other large Southern cities. Only covertly involved on the fringes of the political environment, the upper crust shopped at Goldsmiths, where blacks weren't allowed, and reveled in the elegance of the Peabody Hotel because it represented the high-class Southern charm of the city. Crump's iron hand helped keep the blacks in their place—which was generally any place whites did not want to be.

At the other end of the social spectrum, people like the Presleys thought they were fortunate when they could move from a one-room apartment, where they shared a hall bathroom with three other families, to public housing. Nine months after arriving in Memphis, the Presleys at last had a home again when their application to the Lauderdale Courts housing project was accepted. Compared to their two-room shotgun house in Tupelo, their two-bedroom apartment with its living room, kitchen, and bath made them feel like Southern gentility.

More important to the Presley's future, although they could not have realized it, was the melting pot of music that Elvis found in Memphis. Blacks, whites, rural and city folks, even Yankees, mingled in Memphis, bringing with their cultural diversity a teeming cauldron for music trends.

Before that breeding ground sucked Elvis into its fertile soil, though, the Presleys had to survive. Vernon found work loading and unloading heavy cases of paint, and Gladys, eager to help the family in its upward mobility aspirations, went to work in a curtain factory. Good, steady work, finally. The whole family breathed a sigh of relief.

Once again, Elvis attended an all-white school because Brown v. Board of Education was years over the horizon. At Humes High, Elvis earned decent grades, garnering B's in most subjects, but he once made an F in music. Teachers just didn't respect his talent.

Life wasn't all music, though, and in a close-knit neighborhood, Elvis made friends with a few guys who lived in Lauderdale Courts. Without television and today's electronic gadgets to occupy them, they often rode bikes, went to movies, and played pick-up football. They also liked to hang out in local record stores like Charlie's or Poplar Street Music, listening to the '78 records, made of thick shellac, with only one song on each side. At night, sitting alone on the steps of the apartment, Elvis would strum his guitar, sometimes singing along. Occasionally, a few girls sat with him, entranced by the good-looking, sweet-sounding young man who was so shy he only sang in the dark.

When he wasn't playing his guitar or listening to the radio, Elvis escaped his impoverished home life through comic books, entering an imaginary world where he could create a new environment and a different life. Perhaps the fantasy land in his head gave him the courage to ask a 14-year-old freshman to a prom at the Peabody Hotel. In a new blue suit and a borrowed car, he tasted the future. But he didn't dance at the prom, telling his date he didn't know how.

Life wasn't perfect, but it was good. Vernon bought Elvis a push mower so he and his friends could mow lawns — the four dollars he earned for each lawn helped him buy records, but most of the money he doled out to his parents at the end of each week to help with family needs. And Elvis dreamed. "There must be lights burning brighter somewhere; got to be birds flying higher in a sky more blue."

Elvis kept his dreams to himself at Humes; he didn't share his aspirations or flaunt his talent. In fact, most kids at the high school didn't know he could sing until his junior year. He played around his friends, but he didn't feel comfortable with those he didn't know. Even so, his deep interest in music persisted, and listening to the radio fueled his dreams as he absorbed what music critic Peter Guralnick described as a magic ring, like the one in Aladdin's lamp. The jinni offered a lamp (the radio) dazzling with musical landscapes that had far more than three wishes (musical styles from which Elvis could draw).

Elvis' appetite for music was voracious, and his ears were tuned to pick up new sounds and styles. Dewey Phillips (Daddy-O-Dewey) became one of his favorite disk jockeys (DJs) because he showcased the latest trends, including "Rocket 88," which some say was the first rock'n'roll record. Not unexpectedly, it came out of Sun Records Studio in Memphis.

In a flagrantly segregated city, the music world was colorblind. Restaurants might have sections set apart for blacks, water fountains might be labeled "white" and "colored," and the circus might isolate black people in a back room where they had to peek through the elephants' legs to see the high-wire trapeze act, but music was, to some degree, free of discrimination.

In other venues, zoos, parks, and museums only allowed blacks on certain days, creating resentment at the bigoted injustice, but in their churches blacks found refuge, freedom to express their frustrations and faith in music—sometimes in emotional outbursts and other times in tender tones of yearning. They "felt" their songs, and a farsighted man by the name of Sam Phillips was on the lookout for a white person who could sing like a black one.

Oblivious of Phillips' quest, young Elvis absorbed all kinds of music, gravitating to the styles that hypnotized him. He could *feel* all kinds of rhythms—blues, black gospel, country, and a new tempo that would soon be called "rockabilly." Recognizing that Elvis' passion surpassed his ability, his mama thought he needed more training and asked her new pastor to give him lessons. He was reluctant to teach the backward boy, but Gladys, undeterred, was persuasive, and soon Elvis showed up on Reverend J. J. Denson's doorstep with what Denson described as "a little itty-bitty, Gene Autry-type guitar." And he really couldn't play, Denson discovered. The strings were set so high Elvis couldn't even press them down. Taking pity on him, Denson let Elvis practice on his own small Martin.

By his junior year, Elvis developed more confidence, and whether intuitively or in rebellion, he began to let his hair grow long and applied generous amounts of Rose Oil tonic and Vaseline to keep it in place. Long sideburns added to his cross-country truck driver image. The final transformation came in his clothes as he adopted the dress of R&B musicians. Other kids might be dressed in jeans, but Elvis sported pants, sometimes pink or black, and a black shirt, often adding a well-worn jacket and scarf.

To guide his fashion quest, after Elvis gave money to his parents each week, he wandered down to Lansky's on Beale Street, where the R&B guys purchased their flamboyant clothes. He could only gaze longingly into the windows, but he absorbed style like a sponge. With what little cash he had left from his two part-time jobs, he did what he could to emulate the elegance he admired. As Guralnick observed, Elvis was sounding a clarion bell of style and independence with his dress pants and black bolero accentuated with an ascot, his stiff, shiny hair, and his deliberate demeanor. *Stephen Tyler might have whistled his approval, while Randy Jackson looked at him with a Cheshire cat grin of endorsement.*

Determined to be different, Elvis created an image of the man he wanted to become. He walked with a stagger, dressed with savvy, and bragged to a musician friend, Johnny Black, "Someday I'm going to be driving Cadillacs." And he did; he drove Cadillacs, and he bought dozens of them for his friends and family. He also became Lansky's number one customer in the coming years. But it wasn't quite time. For now, his thirst for wealth could not be quenched.

His hunger for music, though, found sustenance in the All-Night Gospel Singings at Ellis Auditorium, just up the street from where he lived. Most nights, Elvis embarrassed his girlfriend by singing along with the groups, struggling to match both the low and high notes.

For a time, the harmony of gospel quartets became Elvis' mecca. The spiritual force he found there often bled over into other music, but it was in religious songs that he felt exalted and at peace. He was enamored with groups like the Speer Family, the Sunshine Boys, and the Blackwoods, among others, but the Statesmen (led by Hovie Lister with musicians straight out of the backwoods of Sand Mountain) had it all—emotion and showmanship, not to mention a range of voices that could go from one end of a football field to another. They knew how to harmonize the black gospel sound, adding depth and excitement to white music. And, Elvis wasn't put off that their flashy clothes looked like they came from Lansky's. In the future, the flair Elvis absorbed (from the Statesmen and others) into his own wardrobe would help define his stylistic trademark.

When he wasn't at Ellis Auditorium, Elvis didn't lack for music. If he wasn't playing himself, his plaintive tone like a human pulley to young girls, he had his pick of radio stations, which abounded across Memphis, for easy listening. With low transmissions, they popped up on almost every street corner. Radio became Elvis' college of music.

Beale Street, of course, was the "home of the blues," and its version of R&B—faster and more sophisticated—found its way over the airways to Elvis, who was too young to hang out on Beale. But his day was coming. His determination to carve his own image grew, and his love of music flourished in the midst of the Southern musical genres that surrounded him.

Film and pop culture historian Susan Doll saw Elvis as a product of the deep South, noting the music that most influenced and inspired him—gospel, country, blues, and R&B—were indigenous to the region, reflecting its distinctive history. Elvis sang from his roots—a fertile hothouse of races, musical styles, and values. He grew up in an environment, as Doll explains, where blacks and rural white Southerners were able to co-exist in an often tense, racially segregated world while sharing core values and beliefs, including strong family ties, as well as religions that contrasted "earthly suffering and heavenly rewards," focusing on sin and redemption.

# MY WAY

It was only natural, Doll maintains, that the living history of the region came forth in the music and art of rural white Southerners and African Americans; not surprisingly, the common thematic grounds of both races emerged in musical styles and genres.

In an environment of poverty and injustice, Elvis sang "If I Can Dream" from personal experience. He knew what it was to be lonely, to be considered "less than" his fellow man. And he had watched black people, whom he respected and admired as equal, not have the opportunities some white men did. So he dreamed of a better land where his brothers could walk hand in hand. For himself and others, he dreamed that the warm sun would shine hope on everyone. Most of all, he knew that anyone, regardless of race, could "redeem his soul and fly" if he just had the strength to dream.

Whether Elvis realized what he was doing, his growing sense of injustice helped integrate music long before other facets of the culture accepted the end of segregation. But that was in the future.

After he graduated from high school in June, 1953, he had to earn a living, so he took a job at M. B. Parker's Machinist Shop for $36.00 a week ($290 in 2011.) Even helping his parents, he could buy a lot of records and clothes with that kind of money. And, he could plead, deep within his soul, "...please let my dream come true...right now."

# 3
# GOOD ROCKIN' TONIGHT

*Tonight you're gonna know*

*I'm a mighty fine man*

~Buddy Holly

Sam Phillips was looking for a white man who could sing like a black gospel singer. Elvis Presley knew he could sing like no one else (as he told Marion Keisker when he first walked into Phillips' Memphis Recording Studio). And together, the dreams of the two men would come together to create a "good rockin'" time for the world.

Elvis was attracted to the risk-taking Phillips, who after cutting his musical teeth at the innovative WLAY station in Muscle Shoals, Alabama, came to Memphis with his independent, revolutionary ideas about what kinds of music people wanted to hear—and buy.

One of Sam's early unconventional choices was his decision to put out a record by the Prisonaires, a singing group that started inside the Tennessee State Penitentiary in Nashville. Sam risked his career releasing the recording by the prisoners, who had been allowed to travel with an armed guard and a trusty to Sam's little recording studio. The chancy move paid off with strong publicity for Sam and his new studio, Sun Records, garnering coverage in the *Memphis Press-Scimitar*. The Prisonaires "Just Walkin' in the Rain" hit the air about the same time the article appeared, and Elvis undoubtedly thought if five singing prisoners could record a song, he could, too.

Sam, like Elvis, had a goal. And he had intuition and insight about what kind of music people would appeal to listeners. Having arrived in Memphis at the age of twenty-two, Sam already had four years of broadcast experience under his saddle through working at a couple of Alabama radio stations. But he had tired of the era's big band sound, and the country music coming out of Nashville's *Grand Ole Opry* was too smooth. So he started his record company putting out blues' songs.

21

# MY WAY

But Sam had bigger dreams. Good music wasn't limited to whites with money—blacks and whites alike, regardless of their background, shouldn't be deprived of having their music transformed into the American dream. Sam wanted the rhythms of sharecroppers and the wailings of black church choirs to spread across the country. He wanted to rectify how society had overlooked the music imbedded through hardship into the culture of poverty-stricken Southerners. And Sam realized race played a role. It was even more difficult for poor blacks to get their music recognized than it was for poor whites.

Despite his fellow Memphians' aversion to integration, Sam says he "felt from the beginning the total inequity of man's inhumanity to his brother" and recalls wondering what it would have been like to be born black. So he opened Sun Records to record and promote blacks singing cotton-patch blues and their slightly more stylish R&B.

Sam knew Southern racists would never accept the black singers at the level necessary for their music to reach the world, though, so he dreamed of a white man who could capture the essence of field music—"the elements of the soil, the sky, the water, even the wind, quiet nights...." Sam was so sure he knew what he was looking for that he had no doubt he could sense it when the right man opened his vocal cords in his studio. But he didn't.

When Elvis strode through the door of the Memphis Recording Studio (the arm of Sun that made it possible for anyone to record his voice in the days before tape recorders were widely available) and sang "My Happiness," Sam's only comment was "interesting." *(Randy Jackson might have used the word "tentative.")* To be polite, Sam told Elvis he might give him a call sometime. Marion, Sam's assistant, heard more than he did in Elvis' quivering voice. Although Elvis' rendition of the simple ballad held no foreshadowing—not even a hint—of the shake, rattle, and roll power that would later surface, Marion picked up on something. It wasn't the black influence Sam was pining for, and it was tentative, but Elvis' raw emotion, his yearning, came through. Coupled with a sharp nasality, Elvis brought a tone that was deep and full, a craving that cried and crooned, Guralnick notes. Elvis was right when he told Marion, "I don't sound like nobody."

Marion made a note: "Good ballad singer. Hold."

22

She didn't forget Elvis—not because of the strong impression he made on her, but because Elvis wouldn't let her. He pestered her, stopping by the studio regularly, reminding her to let him know if she heard of a band needing a singer. Over and over he came, conveying a sense of neediness Marion couldn't put out of her mind. She sensed he was headed for greatness: "He was," she said in a maternal way, "so ingenuous there was no way he could go wrong."

Elvis' trips to bang his head against Sun Records' wall waned over time, and he expanded his courting. He met Dixie Locke at church and quickly became enamored with her. Dixie's parents were put off by his long, greasy hair and his weird clothes, but Dixie discerned a warmth and genuineness behind the "different" exterior and overcame her family's objections.

Teenagers smitten by first love, they acted like any young couple. Elvis and Dixie hung out, sitting in the park or walking to the Dairy Queen for a milk shake. Occasionally they went to a movie and stopped for hamburgers afterward with the few dollars Elvis kept back from his paycheck, the rest going to his father.

Dixie liked it when Elvis brought along his guitar on their dates. With a little cajoling, he would play and sing for their friends and others hanging out near places like Rocky's Lakeside refreshment stand. Early on, Dixie saw how Elvis' singing of all kinds of music—popular songs, old blues-type songs, and old spirituals—affected people. "You know, it was funny. Right from the start it was as if he had a power over people, it was like they were transformed. It wasn't that he demanded anybody's attention, but they certainly reacted that way—it didn't matter how rough they were or whether they even acted like they were going to be interested or not, they *were*, once he started singing.... People were just mesmerized, and he loved being the center of attention. "

Dixie and Elvis hung out a lot at his house, where she became close to Gladys, who balked at first about the chummy relationship but soon became kindred spirits with her son's first true love. Dixie felt welcome at the Presleys, where she and Elvis could sit for hours listening to Elvis' prized, albeit small, record collection.

Although shy with most people, Elvis opened up to Dixie, telling her about his dreams. He even told her about his unsuccessful attempt to join the Songfellows, an amateur quartet at their church, implying the reason the group turned him down was because the singer they had thought was leaving changed his mind. But Elvis had told his father after the audition, "They told me I couldn't sing." That didn't upset Vernon, who thought Elvis should be glad he had a good job—playing a guitar, he declared, would never make him any money. After the band didn't hire him, even his pastor's son, Jimmy Hamill, told him, "Elvis, why don't you give it up?" Dixie knew the rejection—and the lack of support from his father and his friend—hurt Elvis, but she relates that Elvis shook it off, like "Well, that didn't work out, let's go on to the rest of it."

Undeterred, he auditioned for a spot with Eddie Bond's band. He even had his hair cut for the occasion. But his bullfighter's outfit, complete with a pink shirt, didn't do the trick. After two songs, Bond told Elvis he should stick with driving a truck, "because you're never going to make it as a singer."

Years later, traveling to Hollywood to make *Jailhouse Rock*, Elvis wondered if Bond had changed his mind. "Man, that sonofabitch broke my heart," he exclaimed.

Impatient but confident; fidgety but determined, Elvis waited for his break. When he had all but given up hope that his chance would be through Sun Records, the call came on June 26, 1954—Marion said Sam thought he had a ballad, "Without You," that might be right for Elvis. Could he be there by 3 p.m., she wanted to know. Elvis said he was in the studio before Marion had hung up the phone.

The recording session fell flat, but this time, Sam sensed that with the right song, Elvis could communicate. Still, the afternoon was an abject failure. Elvis later joked, saying "I was an overnight sensation. A year after they heard me the first time, they called me back!" And for a while, it seemed the belated call would be another dead end.

Elvis bombed out on "Without You," but the "something" Sam detected was enough for him to give the young man another chance. He arranged for Elvis to play with two strong musicians, guitarist Winfield "Scotty" Moore and bassist Bill Black, who were currently members of the Starlite Wranglers, a popular Memphis swing band. On July 4th, Elvis auditioned at Moore's home.

Unimpressed with the ducktail-haired kid whose pink pants

24

sported a thin black stripe, the two musicians said the evening didn't get off to a roaring start. "Well, he didn't impress me too damn much," Bill remarked. "Snotty-nosed kid coming in here with those wild clothes and everything." But the singing…"Man…he knocked me out."

Despite the rocky audition, the three young men showed up at the Memphis Recording studio the next day. Sam says Elvis reminded him of some of the blues musicians he had heard — "simultaneously proud and needy." Part of the problem was that even though they tried several songs, Elvis didn't know all of the words to *any* song. Even if he had, Sam couldn't handle the way Elvis bounced all over the place with his voice — sometimes blurting out the words, sometimes drifting into a low, almost pinched, nasal voice. But he always reverted back to a high, keening sound. Sam says it was almost as if Elvis tried to put everything he had ever heard into one song. And it didn't work. Still, the emotion came through — Elvis was communicating a yearning and inconsolable feeling with his voice. It was the same sound Marion had detected more than a year previously.

When everyone had almost given up, during a short break Elvis started fooling around with a blues number he sang in the Courts — "That's All Right Mama." Soon, he was bouncing around in time with the music, interpreting the song with syncopation in an almost-hiccup-like sound. Then Sam engineered some reverberation, giving the sound a slight echo. It was magic. The style Elvis, Sam, and Bill fell into accidentally that night would soon be known as *rockabilly*, described by the historian Doll as a mixture of country music (also called hillbilly) with rhythm and blues, except that the R&B now "rocked" from a shifting back and forth from slow to fast.

Sam knew he had something that night — a style that innovatively integrated and fused African American and rural white Southern genres. He says he felt "like someone stuck me in the rear end with a brand-new super sharp pitchfork."

Doll says Elvis added the "driving rhythm" stemming from mountain music to R&B's hard beat. The result was a combination of country-western music with the blues, reflecting Elvis' wide-ranging personal preferences and his unique affinity with regionally based reverberating sounds. It was new, and it was exuberant; in short, it was original. In Elvis' words: different. According to Sam, his voice was "centuries old." What he did with it was as fresh as a newborn lamb.

Sam's dream was about to come true. He had found the way to attract white people to black music. A few years later, Sam reminisced that while a R&B record would sell to some white teenagers, a barrier existed for many. "There was something in most of those youngsters that resisted buying this music. The Southern ones especially felt a resistance that even they probably didn't quite understand. They liked the music, but they weren't sure whether they ought to like it or not." And that's why Sam came up with his idea of finding white performers who could play and sing in the "same exciting, alive way."

And alive it was. When Sam asked Dewey Phillips to play "That's All Right Mama" on the radio station where he worked, Dewey was at first reluctant, thinking, as Sam thought to himself, "Where are you going to go with this, it's not black, it's not white, it's not pop, it's not country." But he was intrigued and played the song the next night, July 8, 1954, about 9:30 p.m. When his audience went wild, he tried to locate Elvis to come to the studio for an interview, but Gladys told him Elvis was at the movies (probably hiding out because he was nervous that people would make fun of him after his record hit the airwaves). Phillips demanded that the Presleys "get that cotton-picking son of yours down here to the station," adding, "I played that record of his, and them birdbrain phones haven't stopped ringing since." So Vernon and Gladys took off to the theater, walking up and down the dark aisles until they found Elvis and then herded him to the radio station.

Elvis recalls being "scared to death," saying, "I was shaking all over. I just couldn't believe it, but Dewey kept telling me to cool it, [this] was really happening." When Elvis said he was too jumpy to be interviewed, Dewey calmed him down by talking with him about where he went to school. (There was method in his madness—by having Elvis tell the audience he had graduated from Humes, he was letting them know the man who sounded like a black singer was actually white.) After they talked for a while, Dewey thanked Elvis. "Aren't you going to interview me?" Elvis asked. "I already have," Dewey said. "The mike's been open the whole time." Dewey recollected, "[Elvis] broke out in a cold sweat."

GOOD ROCKIN' TONIGHT

Sam might have been sweating, too, but it was not from fear, it was from excitement. He had told Marion a thousand times, "If I could find a white man with a Negro sound, I could make a billion dollars." His dream was about to come true. He was going to have some "good rockin'" with this boy.

But he couldn't put a record out—and he certainly couldn't put the boy on the road—until he had something for the other side. He needed something as rare as a blue moon over Kentucky.

# 4
# BLUE MOON

*Stars shining bright*

*Wish blown high*

~Lorenz Hart

Like "That's All Right, Mama," the song that found its way to the other side of Elvis' first record was a fluke. After three or four nights kicking around a number of songs, trying to find one that matched the excitement of "Mama," the trio hit on an improbable possibility during a break. This time it was Bill Black who started clowning around. In a high falsetto voice, he did a take-off on Bill Monroe's "Blue Moon of Kentucky," a charming waltz known to *Grand Ole Opry* lovers and beloved by hillbilly musicians. Elvis jumped in with his guitar and voice, and then Scotty piped in. Soon, what started as a blues adaptation migrated into a boisterous rendition that reeled into a new, exuberant expression to the timeworn lyrics. Sam once again evolved an echo effect by putting the original recording through a second Ampex machine, creating inflections heretofore unheard. Not only did the echo create a new, exciting sound, but it also disguised mistakes the amateur musicians made as they felt their way along, fashioning new ways to sing old songs. What more could Sam ask for?

By the end of the evening, Sam's coaching had led the timid Elvis and his back-up musicians into a relaxed yet rapid-paced vocal rendition, adding excitement with syncopation and reverberation — features that would become a stylistic hallmark for Elvis.

After Sam was satisfied with the sound, he sent "That's All Right" and "Blue Moon" to a record-producing factory to be pressed into 78 rpm singles and 45 rpm singles.

The instinctive melding of the two distinctly different songs onto his first record defines the electric change Elvis was bringing to popular music. Under the tutelage of Phillips, he combined white country and

28

western and black blues on "That's All Right," originally a blues song written and performed by Arthur "Big Boy" Crudup (who never received royalties from Sun or Elvis and came to resent them, calling Presley his friend "Elvin Preston" in press interviews.) And on the popular, and quintessential, country song by Bill Monroe, Elvis reversed the combination, bringing his love for blues to the hillbilly classic.

Like most of the songs Elvis would record over the next few years, he took proven songs and sang them "his way." In the three weeks following its release on July 19, 1954, the single sold 6,300 copies in Memphis alone, soon climbing to the number three spot on local country-western charts. And that was just the beginning—sales eventually totaled 30,000 across the South.

What Sam dreamed of—and what Elvis turned into reality—had cultural ramifications. Musical integration of black and white sounds came in an era fraught with racial unease. The 1954 Supreme Court ruling that struck down school desegregation didn't go over well in Memphis, as Milton Bowers, Sr.'s comments reflect: The reluctant board of education president nonchalantly responded to the ruling with, "We have been expecting this to happen a long while. But at the same time, we've made no plans because we feel none will be needed." In almost the same breath, the education head declared Memphis would not secede from the Union because of the ruling and would abide by it, while vowing he did not believe white Memphis schools would ever admit blacks. "The white and Negro children of my state are not going to school together." Blacks, hopeful Brown v. Board of Education would change educational opportunities—and other equal rights for their children—weren't about to accept such statements without a fight.

The civil rights activists of Memphis, led by a formidable lady named Maxine Smith, chose their weapons: sits-ins at lunch counters, protests at school board meetings, Black Mondays (during which all black children were kept at home every Monday to put pressure on the school system to admit blacks, crippling the system financially since it was funded on average daily attendance), voter registration drives, shopping center boycotts, and other direct and indirect measures.

While Maxine urged social integration, Sam Phillips pushed Elvis' stylistic integration of voice and performance techniques, which served to blur the black/white culture lines. Although Sam and Maxine may never have met, they were kindred spirits, moving a city, and ultimately a region, toward social change. Like Maxine, Sam received threats and complaints because of his provocative dreams, but just as she refused to surrender her commitment to bring blacks from the back of the bus and from separate but equal schools to true integration, Sam never faltered in his efforts to bring black music into the world of whites.

Musical integration had begun, and Sam hit the road to spread his mission. He had a two-fold plan of action: get Elvis' first single playing on as many radio stations across the Southeast as possible and get Elvis and his band in front of live audiences.

Knowing he had a big task, Sam asked Scotty to serve as the group's manager, scheduling live stage appearances while Sam drove tens of thousands of miles, knocking on doors of disc jockeys wherever and whenever he could find them. He didn't push too hard, but his passion and conviction were often compelling. Sometimes, though, he hit a roadblock. Sam recalls one exchange, talking to T. Tommy Cutrer, a DJ in Shreveport: "If you can give me some play on it, I'd appreciate it. If you can't, I understand." Cutrer resisted, confessing, "'Sam, they'll run me out of town.'"

Even in Tupelo, Elvis' hometown, one radio station manager called the record "a bunch of crap" and declined to play it. But everyone didn't demur, and even though it was lonely and discouraging at times, Sam occasionally got lucky and a DJ spun the record. Bit by bit the record's popularity began to spread, so Sam trudged back to Tupelo and had a heart-to-heart with the station manager about how the world was changing and music was changing with it, adding, "So you might as well start playing it." The manager unenthusiastically conceded. "So we did, and from there on, the music began to change, and change rapidly after that. Younger people started listening to radio stations instead of putting a nickel in the jukebox." He adds, "I look back on it, and that was where it began to turn."

Elvis was in the right place at the right time with the right voice. Sam was the right visionary and the right salesman. Scotty and Bill were glad to be along for the ride.

Back in Memphis, Scotty was setting up appearances, the first at

# BLUE MOON

Overton Park on July 30, 1954. The headliner on the program that night was Slim Whitman, a country yodeler, who boasted several top ten records after having been discovered by Colonel Tom Parker. Slim, along with other stars, including Billy Walker, garnered all of the pre-concert attention. Elvis was so unknown that advance billings called him "Ellis Presley." Unfazed, he was proud to be on the program at all. But he was as nervous as a cat on a hot tin roof.

July 30th dawned hot and humid, typical of mid-summer in Memphis. Dixie remembers Elvis called her four or five times throughout the day and as they drove to the park, she noted his fidgety fingers were drumming more rapidly than usual on the dashboard of the car. Elvis was noticeably scared stiff. Sam describes him as looking "pitiful," or at least "unsure." On stage, Scotty recalls Elvis' knees knocking so loud you could almost hear them. Clutching the microphone with a death-grip, Elvis started tentatively, but his nerves had him so revved up he couldn't stand still, so he moved all over the stage, his leg jiggling as he tapped his foot in time to the music. Elvis' loose-fitting britches had lots of material, and Sam says when he shook his leg, "...it made it look like all hell was going on under there." The crowd went crazy, but initially the self-doubting Elvis thought they were making fun of him. He soon got the message.

"I came offstage, and my manager told me they were hollering because I was jiggling my legs. I went back out for an encore and I did a little more, and the more I did, the wilder they went." He had learned the first lesson of entertainment: connect with your audience and play off its response.

Watching from the wings, Sam Phillips and Bob Neal (who would soon serve as Elvis' manager) observed that Elvis, although naïve and inexperienced, "just automatically did things right." Dixie gazed at Elvis from the front row, and she perceptively realized, "He was doing something so totally *him* that I was not a part of it."

Dewey Phillips now had company. DJ's across Memphis picked up the new Sun record, and Scotty started booking more engagements—everything from schools to civic clubs to the Eagle's Nest (where the Starlite Wranglers played), anywhere someone might be looking for a singing act. It wasn't all peaches and cream—even at the Eagle's Nest,

Elvis was only the intermission act. But every appearance gave Elvis more self-assurance, a better sense of his stage presence. "His movement was a natural thing," Scotty maintains, "but he was also very conscious of what got a reaction. He'd do something one time and then he would expand on it real quick."

Later, as Elvis became the icon of popular culture, critics would debate the genesis of his provocative movements, as well as his overall stage smartness, what Doll calls his "kinetic performing style." But, in the beginning, Elvis just was undeniably doing it "his way."

His way included ensuring his appearance—from his hair to his clothes—fit who he was becoming. As he began to pick up money from the increasing number of performances at local Memphis clubs, as well as a few outside the city, Elvis knew where he wanted to shop. Shyly yet proudly, he strode into Lansky's with a five hundred dollar royalty check from Sun in his pocket. Bernard Lansky remembers the scene like it was yesterday: "'Mr. Lansky,'" Elvis said, handing him the check, "'I wonder if you could cash this for me, I'd like to buy some clothes.'" Lansky's eyes stared at the check in disbelief. Was this the dreamy-eyed kid who had stared in his store windows, the same kid who bought his first shirt there only weeks ago, probably using every cent he owned for that one purchase? With a smile, he told Elvis, "Sure, son." It was Elvis' second purchase from Lansky's, but it was miniscule compared to the dollars dropped by Elvis in his favorite store over the next few years.

Dressed to the hilt, the Hillbilly Cat and the Blue Moon Boys, as they had been christened, took to the road—along with several long-time country music performers. Brazenly but politely, Sam started coaxing Jim Denny, manager of the *Grand Ole Opry* to put Elvis on the big stage. "Give the boy a chance, Jim."

As Dixie watched the blue moon climbing higher and higher, an intuitive foreboding filled her—she was losing Elvis to his fans. But, loving Elvis, she breathed the words of his hit song, "Shine on blue moon. Shine on the one that's gone and made me blue." Even if she lost him forever, Dixie wanted Elvis to rise higher and higher, fulfilling his dream.

# 5
# TOMORROW IS A LONG TIME

*"There's beauty in the silver singing river."*

~Bob Dylan

Recapturing that dynamic feel — black emotion with a white voice — eluded the group over and over as they tried to find new songs to record. Sam recalled, "I had a mental picture, as sure as God is on His throne, I had a mental picture of what I wanted to hear, certainly not note for note, but I knew the essence of what we were trying to do." But he knew the worse thing he could do was to be impatient, "to try to force the issue — sometimes you can make a suggestion just [to change] one bar and you kill the whole song. And sometimes you can be too cocky around people who are insecure and just intimidate them."

Hour after hour, night after night, the trio tried to recreate that sound from their first record — a sound that was taking the country music world by storm. Finally, once again they stumbled into a tune that worked, introducing Elvis' lower register enhanced by Bill Black's ever-thumping bass and Scotty's never-ending guitar rhythm, moving "Don't Care If the Sun Don't Shine" close enough to Sam's vision that he was willing to put it on one side of a record (although some say Elvis never quite made it past Dean Martin's influence to make it "different").

When Sam had all but given up on recapturing the feel of "That's All Right Mama," the right elements fell into place with "Good Rockin' Tonight." The song was a popular blues title written and originally performed by New Orleans native Roy Brown. The popular R&B artist Wynonie Harris made it even more popular among the primarily black R&B audience. Those roots served Elvis and Sam well.

The two shared a lack of prejudice, uncommon in the South. Elvis knew what it was like to be poor, to be looked down on; and the sense of insecurity that came from his impoverished background streamed through his music. What Sam saw and felt, even though he may not have articulated it this way, was encapsulated in words by Guralnick: "[Sam] equated the insecurity that came through so unmistakably in the boy's stance and demeanor with the sense of inferiority—social, psychological, perceptual—that was projected by the great Negro talents he had sought out and recorded."

Elvis and Sam didn't draw the same lines other whites did. Looking white and feeling black came upon them as softly as snow falling on a dark night.

Elvis wasn't the only white singer recording R&B tunes in the mid-1950s, but pop historians Hugh Baker and Yuval Taylor note, "This white country boy wasn't making black songs blander, like Pat Boone or Bill Haley. Instead, he was bringing the joy and excitement he heard in black songs to white America undiluted. And the only way he could do so was pretend to be black." They compare him to Mick Jagger, who ten years later would follow in Elvis' footsteps, updating and continuing "an age-old tradition in American music: blackface minstrelsy." Like other white minstrels, both Jagger and Elvis used exaggeration as part of their technique. "Their aim was to liberate whites from what they saw as their staid, all-too-polite manners and engage them in a kind of entertainment that personified the 'primitive' qualities they saw in blacks: from the casual swagger to the unadorned leer, from the whoops of joy to the jive talk, from the 'riddim' in their bones to the good times in their bottles."

Noting that white rock 'n' roll shifted the minstrel tradition away from poor, uneducated blacks to Americans as a whole, Barker and Taylor (who question Elvis' authenticity) maintain Elvis wanted to make his music all-around appealing. So Elvis avoided stereotypes that most minstrels used, choosing not to blacken his face or wear clothes reflecting poverty. Elvis maintained the image of a polite, though poor, Southern boy in the words he spoke, contrasting with minstrels who sometimes came across as bumbling idiots. In doing so, Elvis broke away from racist shackles associated with minstrelsy, making it possible for his early RCA singles to be popular with both whites and blacks. His voice didn't project either black or white music. Instead, Barker and Taylor avow, Elvis created a new American music that resonated with all who were seeking liberation from the past. Along with freedom, the fresh sound brought a voice of joy and desire to youth yearning for novelty and newness in life and in music.

# TOMORROW IS A LONG TIME

Later, after Sam's influence waned, Elvis freed himself to his broader vision: to be all things to all people. But for now, tomorrow was today — in the homeland of country music.

A week after they had cut their second record ("Good Rockin' Tonight" and "I Don't Care if the Sun Don't Shine"), they were sitting in Sam Phillips' 1951 black Cadillac with Bill's bass buckled on the roof — on the way to appear at the *Grand Ole Opry*. Tomorrow had seemed like a long, long time away when Elvis was strumming his child-like guitar in Lauderdale Courts, but tomorrow had arrived — Saturday, October 4, 1954. Playing at the *Opry* was high cotton — where the big guys performed. Unbelievable. Barely two months after Elvis's first stage performance, Sam's friend Jim Denny had yielded to his plea to "just give the boy a chance."

They would be playing only one song — "Blue Moon of Kentucky," but for the first time in their lives, they would be in the hallowed hall of country music; and they wouldn't be in the audience. On the stage of the shrine of Southern music, Elvis Presley, Scotty Moore, and Bill Black! Like many, they grew up with the Saturday night broadcast from the stage of Ryman Theater and knew by heart the names of all the great performers who had started on the *Opry* stage. They had heard their records and even worshipped the gods and goddesses of the music world who had spring-boarded their careers from Nashville. Would this be *their* place to forever look back on?

They didn't have to wait until tomorrow to find out. The big country music star Hank Snow introduced Elvis, but he couldn't remember his name and introduced him as "a new singer from Memphis." The audience was polite at best — their reaction lukewarm and bland — nothing like the screaming teenagers in Memphis. Still, though Denny declared Elvis wasn't a good match for the *Opry* style, he did concede to Sam, "This boy is not bad." Not high praise but not a total wipe-out. (*The kind of muted criticism that might have come from the lips of Jennifer Lopez if Elvis had been performing on the American Idol stage instead of at the Opry.*)

Elvis worried more about Bill Monroe (who originally recorded "Blue Moon") than judges or critics. He had heard Monroe found the Blue Moon boys' version disrespectful and disgusting. Nothing could have been further from the truth. The gracious Monroe not only complimented their rendition but also told them he was cutting a new recording of "Blue Moon" to emulate their style. Now that was *high* praise. (*Something like Stephen Tyler might have said.*)

Moving on, Sam managed to secure Elvis a spot on the *Louisiana Hayride*, the second most popular country music show in America. This time Elvis would do two shows—one a radio broadcast with a live audience and the second for a theater audience only. Again nervous and fidgety, Elvis leaned into the microphone for the first show and tried desperately to reach his audience, but it was as frigid as the one he had endured in Nashville. The second audience of the night was different—it was filled with college students. More himself in front of kids his age, Elvis jiggled and wiggled, driving his audience into screaming mania. That reaction prompted the *Hayride* manager to offer Elvis and the Blue Moon boys a regular slot on his show.

Time to quit their blue-collar jobs and pump their singing career. But when Elvis told Vernon about his decision, his reaction was like a punch in his gut; his father reiterated his disapproval: "I never saw a guitar player that was worth a damn." Elvis listened, but ultimately he decided to do it "his way." Sam had convinced him they had found "that damn row that hadn't been plowed."

And they hoe'd that row. Within a year, Elvis became so popular Scotty couldn't handle the booking work and all of the appearances, so they signed with a new manager, Bob Neal. Soon, they were touring with the big boys—established country stars like Hank Thompson, the Wilburn Brothers, Mother Maybelle Carter, and Hank Snow. They also made the rounds with contemporary musicians like Marty Robbins and crooners like Faron Young. A few of the younger artists, such as Johnny Cash and Wanda Jackson, saw in Elvis something of themselves—or at least what they wanted to be, in different colors and different tones. And hanging out with Elvis was fun.

Elvis toured with all kinds of country musicians (and even comedian Andy Griffith) because that's where his roots were—in the South and its down-home music. And, by appearing on the same stage with other performers, he set himself apart from their genre. The rows he was hoeing defied description—Elvis was so eclectic he appealed to diverse audiences: country music fans, blues' fans, and blacks as well as whites.

Quickly, his biggest fan base came from a vociferous gaggle of teenage girls whose response approached hysteria. They fell at his feet, pulled his flashy clothes off, and thrilled at mussing his greasy hair when they could get close enough.

Credit must be given to the Blue Moon boys, too, for the wild reception received by Elvis. Scotty's guitar was responsible for the regular repetition of soft and hard accents in the rhythm that became the force of the early records, and Bill played "doghouse bass," a strong style of upright bass (acoustic) that features forceful slapping of the bass strings. The contributions of the two musicians to the new rockabilly sound can't be underestimated according to popular music critics and historians.

Reporters, music writers, and critics of the day struggled to define Elvis' music, failing to perceive that the new genre, volatile and appealing, actually came from the combination of multiple regional sounds. Popular culture historian Doll summarized the difficulty, citing works where critics said of Elvis: "a promising young rural rhythm talent," "a bobbish approach to hillbilly music (half-bob, half Western)," "both country and R&B with an appeal to pop."

"I don't sound like nobody."

Elvis knew that long before his critics realized it. Since he didn't sound like anybody, he didn't have to dress like anybody, either. In his early days of touring, he preferred pleated pants with wide legs, baggy suit coats in wild patterns, snappy two-tone shoes, and garishly patterned ties. No one ever saw him in typical country music garb — Stetson hats, kerchiefs, and embroidered shirts. Reminiscent of his high school days, his stylistic choices looked more like those worn by black R&B artists. To that look, he added eye make-up and a high top, oiled hairstyle swept back into a ducktail. A white man dressed in black clothes with a far-out hairdo. Although Elvis' fashion style evolved over the years, it was at all times "his way."

He was still using his small, child-size, guitar. His movements on stage, though, were moving toward what detractors might have called X-rated. Scotty Moore, describing how Elvis danced all over the place, said the band never knew what to expect. Even worse, fans' screams drowned out the music, and band members had to take their cues to change chords from Elvis' movements. "It was like being in a sea of sound... We were the only band in history directed by an ass," the guitar player recalls.

Scotty evokes the evolution of Elvis' legendary stage moves this way: "He was trying to keep time, but he was doing it with his leg and the britches would start shaking. It was natural... it wasn't made-up. It was just a natural thing." No one denies, though, that Elvis refined his notorious movements based on audience response. The movements may have started out as natural nervousness that instinctively syncopated with the beat of the music, but they evolved into a premeditated performing style as Elvis honed his response to his audience.

Whether natural or faked, on stage Elvis could send a group of teenagers over the edge. One night in 1955, at a baseball park in Jacksonville, Florida, Elvis casually remarked to the crowd of fourteen thousand, "Girls, I'll see you backstage." About half of the girls thought Elvis was talking directly to them, and they took off headlong, pursuing the star into his dressing room. Before they could be stopped, they had torn off his frilly pink shirt, grabbed his socks and shoes, and were working on his pants. The Jacksonville fathers were shocked, leading one pastor, the Rev. Robert Gray of Trinity Baptist Church, to hold a prayer meeting for these misguided girls. He prayed for them, saying that Elvis Presley "had achieved a new low in spiritual degeneracy," and declaring that Elvis, if offered salvation at the prayer meeting, would say "'No Thanks!'" He asked them to pray for Elvis' redemption.

Elvis scorned the preacher when he heard about it. "I feel the preacher was just looking for publicity... I have gone to church since I could walk."

That kind of reaction, both from the audience and those not there, caught the attention of promoter Colonel Tom Parker, an old "carny" (carnival operator) who had managed the career of Eddy Arnold and made a star of Hank Snow. In Elvis, he saw the potential for millions. Soon, in spite of Gladys' instant distrust of the man, he had signed a contract to manage Elvis, beginning a relationship that took both of them to the heights of the music world. With Parker on board, the stage was set for the making of an American Idol.

One Elvis biographer, Pamela Clark Keogh, saw Parker, Phillips, and Presley as a threesome whose dreams intertwined. Elvis' dream waxed eloquent in its simplicity—he wanted to sing in front of people everywhere. Sam Phillips' dream focused on finding a singer who embodied the melting pot of America. Colonel Tom Parker's dream became as crass in its simplicity as Elvis' was eloquent—he wanted to make tons of money. But Colonel Parker had a dark side to his dream. He almost hallucinated about making sure his end of any deal was better than anyone else's.

Within months, on November 21, 1955, the Colonel struck a deal in which Sam sold his Sun contract to RCA for $35,000, (about $325,000 in 2011 dollars) the largest amount ever paid for a recording contract at that time. Did Sam later feel he had been cut out of the "big money"? Not at all, he declared. He was never sorry he sold Elvis. "Listen, as much as I would have loved to have had all the money that Elvis made, or I could have made...absolutely not. You're talking about somebody that grabbed at $35,000 like it was all the money in the world—gosh, to give me a little relief here, while I create other things or try to. It was the greatest blessing that ever happened to me." Back then, $35,000 *was* big money—about 5 times what the average family earned a year. With his buy-out, Sam invested in the beginning of the Holiday Inn hotel chain with his friend Kemmons Wilson. The story goes that Kemmons advised Sam to sell Elvis, saying, "The boy isn't even a professional."

Sam couldn't have gone wrong either way, investing in Elvis or with Kemmons. Besides, he wasn't too sure he could work with Parker, whom he refused to call "Colonel" since it was only an honorary title bestowed by the Louisiana governor, former country music singer Jimmie Davis, for work on his election campaign. The Colonel didn't particularly like the kind of music Sam was promoting, and that didn't set well because Sam believed in the new genre being created, while Parker only believed in Elvis' potential as a moneymaking entertainer. And, he didn't think he could reach that potential with a little record company named Sun Records. The match between Parker and Sam was not made in heaven, and Sam was smart enough to know when to fold.

Elvis moved on with RCA and Colonel Tom Parker. Sam moved

forward, too, and out of his little recording studio at 706 Union Avenue came such greats as Johnny Cash, Carl Perkins, Charlie Rich, and Jerry Lee Lewis.

Along with his new recording contract, Elvis sported a new Martin guitar embellished with his name in black metallic letters on the fret board. He was moving into the big time.

# 6
# GUITAR MAN

*Well, wouldn't ya know,*

*it's that swingin' little guitar man.*

~Jerry Reed

Sun Records launched Elvis like a shooting star, but Sam Phillips didn't have the resources to capitalize on the phenomenon he became. That would take a record company with deep pockets to handle producing and distributing records far beyond the capability of Sun. "[Elvis] was," Jimmy Rodgers Snow said, "the change that was coming to America." Or, as Roy Orbison noted, "There was just no reference point in the culture to compare to it." Of course, he added that Elvis was just a "punk kid, a real raw cat singing like a bird."

Almost everyone recognized Elvis was going places with his guitar, but there was debate in the press and the pulpit as to whether it was to soar in the clouds or wallow in the mud. His fierce energy, his explosive and provocative stage behavior, and his black-music-made-white stirred controversy and shook a conservative American public wherever he went. But to his followers, he was becoming a popular king…a king who needed a bigger stage. It would be the shadowy Colonel Tom Parker who would direct the play.

The star of the play wanted to be big (in his words, "because I want to do something for my folks"), and he knew he had to grow. That growth was described by Bob Neal (in an interview with Jerry Hopkins, who wrote his first Elvis biography in 1971), as "almost exponential, not just in his stage manner, but in an appetite for change and self-improvement that seemed to know no experiential bounds… He soaked up influences like litmus paper…." Elvis constantly studied other performers touring with him, watching from backstage, intuitively grasping what they were doing to reach the audience.

Later, Elvis would say, "I see people all different ages… If I do something good, they let me know it. If I don't, they let me know that, too. It's a give-and-take proposition in that they give me back the inspiration. I work absolutely to them." In other words, he adapted what he did on stage in response to his audience. Tillman Franks of the *Hayride* tours said Elvis went one step beyond most entertainers, who just gave the audience what they had and didn't worry about it. "But Elvis masterminded the situation. He was a genius at it [adapting to the reaction of the crowd]." Provocative and reactive in every way, Elvis created a social revolution with his sexy sneer, his suggestive leg movements, and his sensual voice.

Everywhere Elvis and the Blue Moon Boys performed, crowds went wild. And the money poured in. Elvis replaced the Lincoln he had bought for his first tour with a pink and white Cadillac (his name emblazoned on the door in black) and purchased a pink and white Crown Victoria for his parents. True to his word about wanting to take care of his folks, he also rented a larger home for them. Despite the new-found wealth, Gladys—and Dixie—worried about what the adulation and fame might do to Elvis.

"I know [Gladys] worshipped him, and he did her," Dixie later said fondly, "to the point where she would almost be jealous of anything else that took his time. I think she really had trouble accepting him as his popularity grew. It grew hard for her to let everybody have him. I had the same feelings. He did not belong to us anymore." As her friend Betsy Wolverton remarked, "[Dixie] found it harder and harder to fit into his life."

Elvis himself sometimes wondered where he fit.

The more he was surrounded by people, the more he felt like a stranger. His sense of longing, of wanting to belong in a world that was becoming increasingly foreign to him, came through in the humanness he injected into his songs, much like blacks expressed yearning in their blues music. For someone who had a sincere sense of what he wanted to become, as he became that, Elvis felt more and more uncertain about who he was. Perhaps it was his fear that it wouldn't last, that his popularity would wane and he would have to return to driving a truck. Or, perhaps it simply wasn't what he had dreamed it would be. But he was a star for now, and despite, or maybe because of his uncertainty, he would continue doing it his way, regardless of what anyone thought.

RCA, although paying a record amount for his contract, suspected they had bought a pig in a poke, and Steve Sholes (the highly regarded RCA man assigned to oversee Elvis' recordings) had the formidable job of casting Elvis into the mode of a pop singer, at least for audiences outside the South. In this regard, he was in tune with the Colonel, but he differed in that he supported Elvis' continuing to work in the country and R&B markets where they were popular.

To get Elvis off to a good start as a RCA artist, Sholes asked Chet Atkins to coordinate Elvis' first recording sessions in Nashville on January 10, 1956, a couple of days after Elvis' 21st birthday. By this time, a drummer (D.J. Fontana) had been added to the Blue Moon Boys, and Sholes augmented this group with the talented pianist Floyd Cramer, two of the Speer family members to provide back-up vocals for ballads, and Gordon Stoker, a member of the Jordanaires, for gospel-style harmony. Chet Atkins rounded out the group with his rhythm guitar.

Elvis had been touring for months, and when he arrived at RCA's Nashville Studio, he just kept performing. Sholes and others were shocked at Elvis' approach to recording—he didn't need to act like he was in front of an audience; that wasted time. His unorganized, chaotic way of recording a take, playing it back, discarding it, and starting again ad nauseum, left Sholes shaking his head in dismay. In New York, RCA executives became disconcerted when they heard the first takes—they didn't sound anything like the Sun records still topping the charts and sending listeners into spasms. Adding supporting vocalists and more musicians altered Elvis' sound, and they weren't too sure that was good.

Still, in his first recording session with RCA, Elvis cut Ray Charles' "I've Got A Woman," as well as "Heartbreak Hotel" and "Money Honey." The other two cuts, on a second day, were "I'm Counting on You" and "I Was the One." Despite the initial discomfort of Sholes and his bosses, "Heartbreak Hotel" made the charts, within two months becoming the label's No. 2 seller. The eerie song with its exaggerated echo effect eventually gave Elvis his first gold record when it climbed to number one on both the *Billboard* singles chart and its country chart, not to mention holding the number three spot on the R&B chart for several weeks. Elvis' eclectic music appealed across diverse audiences.

# MY WAY

After the recording session, Elvis did a quick Texas tour before taking a plane to New York on Wednesday, January 25, 1956, two days before the first of his Nashville studio recordings, "Heartbreak Hotel," was to be released. The trip marked his first appearance on Tom Dorsey's CBS television program, *Stage Show*. In his fancy pants with shiny stripes and colorful tweed jacket, the rising star from Memphis looked like a redneck compared to the classy elegance of Ella Fitzgerald and Sarah Vaughan, who shared the stage that night. What no one knew is that Elvis had made a special trip to Lansky's to make sure he was appropriately attired for the Big Apple. He had informed Mr. Lansky he had outgrown his trademark pink and black and was ready for something more sophisticated. Still, he wanted to make a statement—to look different—so the orange raw silk blazer and the ivory button blouson cuff Lansky suggested would be a good start. A little extra mascara for the camera wouldn't hurt, either.

For "Shake, Rattle, and Roll," Elvis shot out on stage but quickly boomeranged—his first song fell flat with the small Dorsey audience made up mostly of servicemen and others wanting to escape the wintry weather. When Elvis started banging his guitar, flailing his hips, arms, and shoulders at the same time, the people watching the strange-looking character on stage stiffened their spines. Eyes started to roll as Bill Black banged his guitar, then straddled it. (*Randy Jackson would have had a few words to say about that, probably telling Elvis he wasn't at Disney's Animal Kingdom.*)

Naked without his screaming fans, Elvis never lost his confidence— he just segued into another song and another, enjoying the moment. Nevertheless, it wasn't the dramatic launch Elvis and the Colonel had planned. Doll described him as "wild, raw, and alien" compared to the exquisitely dressed, polished performers who preceded him on the stage.

Before Elvis' next Dorsey show, a recording session with RCA took place in New York, where Sholes decided to cut back on the number of musicians, adding only boogie-woogie piano player Shorty Long to the Blue Moon boys. Sholes took more control this time, directing the selection of fast, fiery sounds RCA thought would keep Elvis flaming hot with his fans. The outcome: Elvis' version of Carl Perkins' "Blue Suede Shoes" and Little Richard's "Tutti Frutti," as well as Arthur Crudup's

# GUITAR MAN

"My Baby Left Me." As usual, Elvis only recorded songs others had already put on acetate.

The seven tracks recorded in Nashville and New York ended up on a long-playing (LP) album that also included five songs recorded by Sun Records but not previously released. Hitting the market on March 13, 1956, the album climbed to number one on *Billboard's* Top LP chart and topped out as RCA's first million-dollar album by a single artist. The pig in the poke produced winners.

Despite Elvis' phenomenal success on the road, his vinyl popping off shelves, and teenagers plunking change into jukeboxes across the nation, the Colonel knew television was the key to ultimate success. He reasoned more people would see Elvis on one television show than on a lifetime of *Louisiana Hayride* stages. Unfazed by the lack of initial interest from Arthur Godfrey's *Talent Show* and the cool reception on Dorsey's *Stage Show*, the pushy promoter determined to showcase Elvis on coast-to-coast broadcasting, something that had not been possible until the early 1950s. Fortunately, Dorsey had contracted for four shows on the front end.

The rest of the Dorsey shows mended the initial fractured image from Elvis' first appearance. He dressed more conservatively, and with an audience more in line with his style, he played to them in the same way he had found so successful. He did have one song fall short, "Heartbreak Hotel," because the Dorsey brothers' orchestra added an arrhythmic arrangement that didn't give Elvis his wiggle cues.

Justin Tubb, son of Ernest Tubb, was there for this show and noted television couldn't capture the Elvis that fans loved on the road. He called Elvis "a diamond in the rough." Some people liked their diamonds polished, and for them, Elvis' "magnetism or charisma" was lost in the sounds and moves they couldn't fathom as real music and proper dancing.

After the last Dorsey show, a reporter asked Elvis about his shaking and wiggling, which was continuing to stir up controversy. Elvis said he knew CBS hadn't wanted him to jump around on stage so much, but it was just the way he performed; it was just the way he did it. It was the only way he knew. It was *his* way.

Elvis was glad to get back on the road again. In front of frenetic fans, when he gave his all, people appreciated him. Coming off stage, soaked and dripping, having put everything he had into his performance, he knew he had not only connected with his audience — he had communicated with them. They felt what he felt, and his dream was being fulfilled. It was a hard life, though. At one show in Jacksonville, Florida, Elvis fell out cold on the stage. Later that night, a doctor told Elvis he was "doing as much work in twenty minutes as the average laborer does in eight hours." He added that Elvis needed to slow up, or he would end up having to take off a couple of years to recover.

Elvis checked out of the hospital the next morning and never looked back. Slowing down was not an option. At *Hayride* the next week, Scotty watched Elvis create an explosion with "Heartbreak Hotel," saying, "It had been wild before that, but it was more like playing down at your local camp, a home-folks-type situation. But now they turned into — it was different faces, just a whole other.... That's the earliest I can remember saying, *What's going on?*"

Gladys knew what was going on, and she was worried. Dixie discerned, too, that Elvis had drifted out of her life. Although he would always love and respect Dixie, Elvis had moved on and there was no turning back.

Although Elvis was rarely home, he hadn't forgotten his parents, buying them a new house — seven rooms, a pretty nice place, he said proudly. Because his mother worried about him so much, he called home every day to let her know he was okay. The mother-son connection remained rock solid.

In an era before media saturation, before MTV, YouTube, iTunes, Pandora, satellite radio stations, iPhones and MP3 players, going on the road was the only way to keep Elvis in front of his fans when he couldn't get on television. So, the road shows continued. Scotty remembers the routine: "We'd pull into some town, go to the hotel room, and get washed up or go right to the auditorium or movie house, and after we played our shows, we'd get back in the cars and start driving to the next town. We never saw newspapers... and we didn't hear much radio, because we drove all night, slept all day. All we knew was drive, drive, drive." D.J. Fontana adds, "It was like being in a fog." It didn't take long to put 100,000 miles on a car. An earthquake had hit America, and the tsunami that followed in its wake created waves across the ocean as far as Europe. Soon, the Beatles would come calling, wanting to meet the king in person.

Between concerts, the Colonel managed to squeeze in two appearances for Elvis on *The Milton Berle Show*, as well as a screen test with producer Hal Wallis. His first appearance on Milton Berle's variety show was broadcast from the *USS Hancock* while it was docked at the San Diego Naval Station, and the publicity following it paled in contrast to the storm of controversy that blasted Elvis following the second appearance on June 5, 1956, five months later. Performing "Hound Dog" for the first time on television, Elvis chose not to play his guitar, thrusting his provocative movements even further into the forefront. Encouraged by screaming fans, in the final chorus Elvis slowed the song down to a blues tempo, thrusting his hips toward the microphone stand he was grasping as he balanced on the balls of his feet. The sensual effect sent fans into a frenzy and critics into crying foul. The *New York Herald Tribune* reflected the growing concerns across America, calling Elvis "unspeakably untalented and vulgar."

While Elvis and the Blue Moon boys were traveling in a fog, disconnected from the world not part of their appearances, their fans were immersed in events that generated uncertainty. It was the height of the Cold War, and the beginning of a civil rights movement that many feared. Elvis and musicians like him were ripe targets for a threatened society.

Rallying around the media, parents and religious groups roundly condemned Elvis, making him the villain for all teenager misbehaviors, transferring fears from the larger world to a more personal environment. A whole generation was being influenced and driven into parental rebellion by a greasy-haired kid.

It seems every generation has targets when its moral fiber is under attack. For Elvis, deep-rooted issues in our society and culture created a clamor because of the vast abyss in America that divided young from old, black from white, working class from middle class, rural Southern culture from mainstream sophistication. Elvis defied not only political correctness but also common decency, according to some critics. In their attacks, they denounced his burlesque-like sensuality on stage and scoffed at his Southern background and music genres. Some authority figures believed Elvis was going to lead a whole generation into juvenile delinquency. In an interesting twist, the pop culture historian Doll points out that no one seemed concerned about the "depraving" effect the swinging hips and breast-revealing tops of Marilyn Monroe, Jayne Mansfield, and other sex symbols were having on young men. Teachers, preachers, and parents must have thought young ladies needed more protection from evil influences than young men did since only Elvis was under constant fire. Of course, no one else had rabid fans who tore their clothes off, either.

Steve Allen wanted Elvis on his show, but he was mindful of the concern about Elvis' negative influence. After a press release declaring, "Elvis Presley will not be allowed to bump and grind," Allen followed up by having Elvis sing "Hound Dog" to a live basset hound. Dressed in a tuxedo, standing next to the floppy-eared dog and looking into its eyes as it gazed curiously at him from the pedestal where it sat, Elvis was a good sport. Later, though, Elvis told friends he felt humiliated. Moreover, his fans weren't happy. While Maxine and her fellow civil rights activists were picketing shopping centers in Memphis, the next day Elvis disciples picketed NBC-TV, carrying placards reading, "We want the gyratin' Elvis." The more television tried to tame Elvis the Pelvis, the more his fans cried for the unshackled Elvis.

That's what they got when Elvis appeared for the third time on the *Ed Sullivan Show*. The only problem was that they couldn't see the wiggling since Sullivan had instructed the cameramen to shoot Elvis only from the waist-up. A producer on the show, Marlo Lew, claimed a good reason existed for the censorship: It appears a rumor had been spread that Elvis had placed a Coke bottle down his pants for the appearance so that when he bounced around, an obscene impression would show through his pants. Another rumor related that Elvis planned to place an empty toilet paper roll down his pants to produce a similar impression. Truth or legend? Likely legend, but no one knows. But it was the first and only time the waist-up rule was enforced. From then on, "that swingin' little guitar man" did it his way, and it was all captured on film. Giant crowds of people followed wherever he performed, eager to get on the dance floor. May Axton, the advance woman for road tours, said the Colonel had "dollar marks in his eyes."

And well he should have. Not too much later that year *Variety* announced in a front-page banner headline that Elvis had become a millionaire in one year. With more than ten million records sold, he had captured almost two-thirds of RCA's entire sales for singles that year. "Don't Be Cruel" hit the three million mark, and "Hound Dog" made it to two million. Both made it to number one on all three charts

# 7
# SHAKE, RATTLE, AND ROLL

*I believe it to my soul you're*

*The devil in nylon hose*

~Big Joe Turner

Memphis sits atop the New Madrid Fault Zone, the most active fault east of the Rockies. Its most active period occurred in 1811-12, when some of the largest earthquakes in North America's history caused the mighty Mississippi River to briefly flow backwards, leading to the formation of Reelfoot Lake.

Attempting to create a civil rights earthquake in the mid-1950s, Maxine Smith became "the most loved and the most hated" voice in Memphis. On one side, people "hated her for her outspoken and tenacious advocacy for those rights;" on the opposing flank, "her followers loved her for her unwavering commitment to ensure the rights of African Americans." Writing in the *Commercial Appeal Mid-South Magazine,* Anita Houk avowed Maxine took whatever criticism she must: "Her thunder has inflamed rivals and inspired supporters. It has made her the most loved and most despised woman in Memphis. She has been spat on and bowed to, cursed and applauded, called everything from crusader to fiend."

Memphis was also Elvis Presley's epicenter, and the earthquake that began with his first hit from Sun Records sent aftershocks for thousands of miles over an extended period of time. Like Maxine, his voice was the most loved and the most despised, but its reach was far greater, crossing not just state lines and reaching past the South, but beyond national and international borders. All because some people thought Elvis had "the devil in his nylon hose."

After finally winning over the crowd on Tommy Dorsey's show and having his first album with RCA become their top-selling ever, Elvis rolled into Las Vegas for his first visit to sin city expecting to be received like an "atomic powered singer," as the Colonel promoted. At his first show, Elvis launched into the song that had been an unequivocal hit on Dorsey: "Blue Suede Shoes;" but, like the aftermath of a summer storm, the heavy air was starkly silent. Little old ladies in hats and fur coats peered at Elvis like the devil incarnate. Their husbands, afraid to move, knew they were in terrible trouble for bringing their wives into the devil's den. An electrical storm ensued, but this time it was not on the stage.

Shaken, for the first time Elvis wondered if he was just a shooting star, a brief flame burning out before it finished lighting the night sky.

*Variety* saw what had happened: "For teenagers, he's a whiz; for the average Vegas spender, he's a fizz." *Newsweek* magazine described Elvis' performance in Vegas as "somewhat like a jug of corn liquor at a champagne party."

*Variety* and *Newsweek*'s criticism came out mild compared to the attacks after the *Milton Berle Show,* assaults that continued for years. *Time* magazine surmised Elvis "might possibly be classified as an entertainer, or, perhaps, just as easily, as an assignment for a sociologist." *Look* magazine thought Elvis' wiggles resembled "a peep show dancer. Onstage, his gyrations, his nose wiping, his leers are vulgar." *Life* asserted Elvis "uses a bump and grind routine usually seen only in burlesque."

*Time* avoided sexual imagery but reported, "His body takes on a frantic quiver, as if he had swallowed a jackhammer." *Illustrated* alleged he looked "as if a whole empire of ants had invaded his pants." "If Elvis did that on the street," a Los Angeles policeman maintained, "we would arrest him."

John Sharnik of *House and Garden* magazine offered insight into the reason behind the criticism: "...adults were angered that a distinctive [teen] audience exists at all, that within our own society there is a large, well-defined group whose standards of taste and conduct we find baffling and even terrifying... Youth is almost a national cult." What many saw as an evil influence, Sharnik described as nothing more than "background music in the war between the generations."

Elvis couldn't understand what all the fuss was about. "I know that I get carried away with the music and the beat sometimes. And I don't quite know what I'm doing. But it's all rhythm and the beat—it's full of life. I enjoy it. The kids understand it. It's the newness. I think older people will grow to understand...."

The fear of the devil crossed the ocean where Russian teenagers, infatuated with the king, watched in disbelief as their Communist government outlawed the sale of rock records and more specifically, "condemn[ed] Elvis as a capitalist pawn." Russian capitalists weren't to be deterred—they found a way to cut records on discarded hospital X-ray plates and then sold the bootlegged records to the teens ravenous for music that spoke to their fettered souls. Again, Elvis was mystified: "I don't see how any type of music would have any bad influence on people. When it's only music... I mean how would rock 'n' roll music make people rebel against their parents?"

Susan Doll believed the basis for unadulterated criticism of Elvis stemmed partly from disrespect for anything arising out of the South. The music industry was particularly resentful of the success of someone so different from conventional musicians. The three genres blended by Elvis—R&B, blues, and country western—all originated in the South. Worse, they were at the opposite end of the spectrum from the "smooth-sounding pop ballad" revered by tastemakers in New York, Los Angeles and Chicago.

Prejudice against the "hard sounding, beat-driven, and emotionally raw" music woven from the indigenous Southern genre exposed deep-seated regional issues. Tin Pan Alley, the New York district from 28th Street between Fifth Avenue and Broadway in Manhattan, was losing its dominance in the music industry, and an upstart young man with swivel hips threatened its existence. Doll explains the underlying factors: Because many of the songwriters associated with Tin Pan Alley had immigrated from Europe, or at least their parents or grandparents had, the style they were most comfortable with—the style they promoted—was more mainstream, leaning toward Broadway musicals and Hollywood songwriters. Fusing country westerns, R&B, and blues, as Elvis did, was heresy. The three genres should stay distinct. Of course, behind the self-righteous indignation was a general dislike and put-down of anything from the South. Replacing the smooth sound of pop ballads with the ragged, rhythmic sound tied to enflamed emotions evoked charges of musical sacrilege—it was almost primeval, uncivilized.

Tangentially tied to black music, the controversy created around Elvis could be compared to the Civil War, but this time the central conflict was between generations, not races. The unprecedented battle between parents and teenagers dwarfed other explanations for the repercussions of Elvis' music as generational rebellion became entangled with the new genre. Granted, a minority of historians attach racism to the controversy, believing Elvis' television performances exposed their children to a culture they considered untamed. However, most popular culture observers and historians think the intense resistance to Elvis had more to do with his Southern poverty roots and his "white trash" predilection to weird attire, his frenetic performance style, and his hillbilly accent. Elvis' popularity posed a danger to cultural values imbedded in urban white America.

While the criticism of Elvis' accent, his flashy clothes, and his funky hair were of concern, it was his movements on stage that fueled the fires. Even so, Barker and Taylor observe, Elvis' voice held the key to the whole man, to the persona that roused a revolutionary response across America. Most critics failed to notice that, inspired by Elvis' success and popularity, and moved by the sheer joy of his performances, other rock 'n' roll singers replicated not only his moves and down-South accent but also his vocal maneuvers. Record producers were looking for artists that could reach an audience like Elvis, could sound like him: his ability to move like a glider plane from his lower range to an artificially high voice—adding, when they could, his hiccupping, not to mention the stutter that sometimes smudged his words. And they found them, pushing people like Roy Orbison, Charlie Rich, Wanda Jackson, and Carl Perkins into the limelight. Numerous other Elvis imitators were spawned, and they swam down the rivers of America's new music.

Sun's publicist said they were all totally nuts. "I think every one of them must have come in on the midnight train from nowhere. I mean, it was like they were from outer space."

They were all actors, but so was Elvis. "Elvis could imitate anybody," according to one of his early girlfriends, Barbara Pittman. "He could do Hank Snow, Dean Martin, Mario Lanza, Eddy Arnold, the Ink

Spots, anybody." Of course, as Barker and Taylor point out, Pittman is referring to Elvis' voice—not his controversial stage movements. He knew exactly what he was doing with his voice: Instinctively, he infused snarls in his voice and sneers in his smiles at a place where they added drama to a song. But it was all an act. The arrogance he assumed wasn't real. It was for effect. The air of self-importance that came across in his singing was in contrast to the true Elvis, who emerged in interviews, when he became the boy his mama raised, deferential and shy.

Interestingly, it is the combination of genres, notwithstanding his vision and desire, that sets Elvis apart. That amalgamation also set him up to be accused of being inauthentic. If he was simply mixing old music in new ways, he wasn't an original, according to a small number of music critics. He was just putting old wine in new skins. Some accused him of not being true to his roots, of artifice rather than art.

By breaking with past styles, even in clothing, rock 'n' roll singers like Elvis abandoned their real world and created an artificial one where their actions—typically in promiscuity and partying—violated their moral codes. The world they created allowed uninhibited behavior and outlandish appearances on and off stage.

Ironically, the very reasons critics cite when calling Elvis inauthentic are the ones many other music reviewers use to explain why Elvis remains a legend. Singing his way, performing his way, even if it evolved from an innate ability to read his audience and react to it, didn't detract from his authenticity. He put the Elvis stamp on everything he did, every song he sang. "Elvis' style—so inherent in him—worked because it was authentic. He was inventive, not an invention," observed Pamela Keogh.

One can imagine *American Idol*'s judges entering this debate, since they often tell some singers to be true to themselves while, seemingly in contradiction of this admonition, criticize others for not venturing into "unsafe" places—genres outside their preferred style.

Elvis represented change, and it was as authentic as a patchwork quilt pieced together from scraps of the past. Reverencing the past by weaving it into the future made Elvis more, not less, authentic.

In early essays, Presley biographer Guralnick fashioned Elvis in two ways: First, as a singer who emotionally delivered songs he cared about "without barrier or affectation." He says Elvis never again evoked the soul and vitality of his first sessions at Sun, never recapturing the innate joy that filled the studio with pure passion and energy. Those moments in time were never repeated because they were instinctive and pure. Elvis' RCA records became almost self-parodies, ridiculously silly. As his popularity, and the demands placed on him, grew, Elvis changed. His early innocence and absence of self-consciousness, where he threw everything he knew about life into a song, turn into a caricature of the early Elvis, to excesses in music and stage performances.

People closest to him say Elvis "felt" every song he sang. He forged an identity with new interpretations of old songs, a sensual style of performing, and "way-out" clothes. He was part and parcel of a generation born in poverty who now found disposable income burning in their pockets. He dreamed with them, saw the need for social integration, and embodied their vision to step outside the music and tastes of their parents. Inexplicably, the parents eventually found themselves drawn to some of Elvis' later music. Elvis was right: older people grew to understand.

Elvis crossed generations then and now, but he also cut through chasms separating people — race, age, class. He embodied the American dream. Whether that was art or artifice may be debatable, but his imprint on the music world lives on.

Before that happened, though, the Colonel had to deal with the stage shenanigans of his rising star or the critics were going to eat him alive or the fans were going to pull him apart. Mob and press control just weren't working.

The solution: Pull Elvis off the road and put him on the big screen. People were "doing [him] wrong" and the Colonel would "save [his] doggone soul."

# 8

# ANY DAY NOW

*Oh any day now,*

*Oh, oh, oh*

~Bob Hilliard

Elvis loved women. Lots of them... All of them... He loved Hollywood movie stars, country girls, and everything in between. But few question that he loved the woman he was with at any given moment with his whole heart. He wooed them, played with them, and then moved on. But while he was there, his girl friends were in heaven. Known as a great kisser, he was also good in bed if his movements on stage were any foretaste. Even so, Elvis respected his woman, and with the young ones, he didn't go beyond kissing and a little touching. Some say it was because of his deep respect for his mother. He might come close, but he usually didn't go all the way. With true Southern respect, he always stopped before the girl had to say no.

In Memphis, Vegas, Hollywood, or on the road, women were part of who Elvis was and what he did. Sometimes they traveled with him; other times they waited for him back at home, hoping he would call, sitting by the phone in those days of a monolithic Ma Bell, before answering machines and voicemail. And for sure there wasn't any call waiting, so a girl knew to keep her line open in case Elvis called.

June Juanico typified the waiting girl, although when Elvis appeared on her doorstep one July night in 1956 to escape the heat of his critics and the onslaught of his fans, she was caught off guard—he hadn't even called to say he was coming. In fact, she hadn't heard from him in months. Elvis had taken three weeks off after performing for a packed house in his hometown; and Biloxi, where June lived, seemed the perfect place to unwind. Despite having no advance notice, June quickly rearranged her schedule and devoted herself to Elvis. She had already learned that, "If you were going to date Elvis...it was always his schedule, you had to keep your calendar entirely free at all times, and you could not ever, *ever* call him."

Biloxi was just what Elvis needed. He went deep-sea fishing with June's mother and Eddie Bellman and had so much fun he called his parents, insisting that they join him. Money to burn, he rented a villa at the Gulf Hills Dude Ranch in exclusive Ocean Springs—away from the relentless crowds who tracked him down at the beach. Elvis loved his fans, but the pink lipstick messages on his Cadillac had begun to fray on his nerves.

On the water with his parents and June, Elvis felt more peaceful than he had in months. The elder Presleys relished the time with Elvis, and Gladys felt relieved to see him acting normal. She even made him peanut butter and banana sandwiches to eat while they puttered along, trolling for fish. She liked June, and she could see Elvis was taken with the girl. Getting married might calm Elvis down, she reasoned, and she hinted to June that she might be the right girl, although she also warned her to avoid letting the Colonel know she was serious about Elvis. "You know how he feels, especially about marriage."

Elvis cautioned June, too. He had promised the Colonel at least three years, and he couldn't go back on his word, so it would be that long before he could even think about marriage and having children.

Despite the restrictions on their relationship, Elvis and June had a good time. Well-matched, they both loved to cut up and fool around, and she even liked to sing. In her mind she was as good or better than he, saying she told him that "most of his records sounded like he was singing in a tin can." With the right music, though, she thought his voice might be wonderful since they often sang together, songs like "Side by Side," "Back in the Saddle Again," and "Let the Rest of the World Go By," as they rode around, Elvis singing the lead and June harmonizing with the tenor.

In addition to sharing a love for music, June brought out Elvis' spiritual side. She was the first to introduce him to *The Prophet,* by Kahlil Gibran. They read it together, and Elvis was hooked. As he had with Dixie, Elvis shared his innermost thoughts with June. One night, as they were sitting on a pier, he asked June to look up at the moon, telling her to relax and remove everything except what she was seeing from her mind. If she would do that, he encouraged, she could "float in the space between the moon and the stars." He had been doing it since he was a little boy, he admitted. But he didn't tell many people because they would think he was crazy. Only his mother really understood. Now, he was sharing it with June.

The weeks flew by, and a couple of times Elvis returned to Memphis on business, although June wondered if the "business" might be his current Memphis girlfriend, Barbara Hearn. She knew better than to question Elvis, though. He didn't like that—his women had to expect that they would have to share him. He also expected them to stay by his side, and June didn't always comply. She recalls Elvis complaining, saying, "'Other girls I've dated are always right next to me. They act like they're proud to be with me. If I say something, they listen. If I want to say something to you, I have to find you first.'" June knew what she was doing—sometimes she disappeared intentionally, just to see if Elvis noticed. She had not forgotten that when they first met, he had told her he liked her because she wasn't like other girls. So she wasn't going to fit the mold of being at his beck and call.

The idyllic days with June came to a close when the movie tryout Elvis had had in New York resulted in an offer to be in a western, *The Reno Brothers*. It was just what the Colonel ordered. He hadn't forgotten how bad the free-for-alls had gotten before he pulled Elvis off the road.

Whether the adverse publicity following his Memphis performance just before his visit to June was the final straw or ongoing criticism like the Florida preacher who denounced Elvis a year earlier as achieving "a new low in spiritual degeneracy," the Colonel knew "any day now" a "blue shadow [might] fall over town." His "wild beautiful bird," the one with moneybags under its wings, might not just fly away; it might fall from the sky.

While the Colonel's concerns reflected his obsession with money, Gladys Presley's uneasiness came from a mother's heart. For months, her apprehension had been steadily building. At the Municipal Auditorium Arena in Kansas City, Missouri, fans had rioted on May 24, smashing D.J.'s drums and Bill's stand-up bass. D.J. ended up in the orchestra pit, and Elvis sprinted to a waiting car 20 minutes into his concert. Gladys worried Elvis would be killed, but she also feared he might simply die on stage. Her nightmare was that it would be the latter. Her little boy was going to end up dead if somebody didn't slow him down. It could happen "any day now."

Gladys' fears had magnified at the Memphis concert that followed the one in Kansas City and preceded Elvis' escape to Biloxi. But this time her foreboding went beyond his physical safety. Elvis' keening sound — woeful and shrill — filled the air as he kicked off with "Heartbreak Hotel," followed by "Mystery Train" and "I Got a Woman." By the time he got to "Hound Dog," he was completely lost in his music; it was as if he had left his body, abandoning it to be controlled by an unknown spirit. His mother was terrified by this loss of her son — Elvis had been transported into someone she didn't know. As Elvis slipped from a whirling, hip-grinding beat to a slower, distorted sound that was almost a growl, the teenage girls were carried with him, their screams otherworldly. In a state similar to poltergeist, they threatened to eat him alive. Elvis biographer Keogh sums the performance up: "Elvis was black and white, country and rock, male and female. Beyond definition, he brought to the light what others saved for the dark." She concludes that Elvis had no problem taking other people where he wanted to go — their emotions meshed with his, and they felt every move and nuance of his voice and body.

To save the wild bird, it had to be caged. Hollywood was the perfect place to pen Elvis up, away from the maniac girls.

But the filming didn't begin for another six months. Elvis couldn't sit still, and the Colonel, despite the potential for more negative publicity and near-riots, wasn't willing to let his money-making machine stay idle that long. To keep the dollars flowing, he scheduled Elvis for a tour in Florida. With his usual charm, Elvis convinced June's mother and father to let her accompany him, assuring them she would be well chaperoned. With Elvis' friends and cousins constantly nearby, they were never alone anyway.

The newspapers went wild with June's appearance in Miami, and a reporter trapped her, manipulating her into talking about her relationship with Elvis. The Colonel went ballistic when he read the article, and his anger exploded when he subsequently read a quote by June's mother that Elvis and June would be getting married in three years. Elvis was torn—he did love June even if he didn't know whether he would ever marry her, but he felt beholden to Colonel Parker for his growing success.

The Colonel's worries shifted when newspaper articles became more and more vicious. The *Miami News* reported, "Elvis can't sing, can't play the guitar—and can't dance. He has two thousand idiots per show," adding that Elvis shook his pelvis like a striptease babe. Elvis became incensed at someone calling his fans idiots. "Because they're somebody's kids. They're somebody's decent kids, probably...raised in a decent home, and he hasn't got any right to call those kids idiots." He was even angrier when a reporter implied his gyrations on stage originated from his being a "Holy Roller." Without losing a beat, Elvis let the "idiot" know being a member of the Assembly of God Church did not make him a "Holy Roller." Besides, he added, "My religion has nothing to do with what I do now."

The breaking point might have been when people began to hiss at June and gossip about her, calling her a whore. Or, it might have been in Jacksonville, Fla., when Judge Marion Gooding, in an effort to avoid repetition of a previous year's performance, told an Optimist Club she was preparing warrants to charge Elvis with impairing the morals of minors. The good judge would issue the warrant if Elvis once again "put obscenity and vulgarity in front of our children." Elvis outsmarted the moralistic judge, replacing his gyrating leg with the wiggle of his little finger. After the show, he told June, "Baby, you should have been there. Every time D.J. did his thing on the drums, I wiggled my finger, and the girls went wild. I never heard screams like that in my life. I showed them sons of bitches—calling me vulgar."

Elvis, glad to get out of Florida, set off to New Orleans for the last leg of the tour and then on to Memphis to rest for a couple of days before heading to Hollywood. He was as relieved to get away from his fans for a while as the Colonel was to get him off stage. The caged bird would still be able to sing, but audiences would have to wait for the theatre release to hear him. No more live performances for a while.

Elvis was excited—any day now he was going to be a movie star.

# 9
# LOVE ME TENDER

*All my dreams fulfill. . .*

~Ken Darby

Elvis may have been thinking about one of his lovely ladies when he sang, "Love Me Tender," but girlfriends weren't part of fulfilling his dreams. Only starring in movies could make his real dream come true. Singing stars climbed into the limelight and then faded away, Elvis reasoned; those who lasted became serious movie stars—like Frank Sinatra and Bing Crosby.

While Elvis agreed with the Colonel that he needed to maintain his appeal to audiences while slowing down on the controversial, sometimes riotous, road tours, they saw his role on the big screen differently. Elvis wanted to be a dramatic actor—not a singing one. The Colonel saw movies as a vehicle to sell more records and market Elvis merchandise.

The old carny was wallowing in the opportunities that Elvis' popularity made possible. Elvis fans were buying his records at an unprecedented pace, and royalties were flowing. Capitalizing on this "Elvis mania," the Colonel was merchandizing him like no other pop culture figure. He had linked up with a well-known, highly successful merchandiser named Hank Saperstein, and teenagers everywhere were lapping up the result: Elvis Presley lipstick in colors named after his popular songs—Hound Dog Orange, Tutti Frutti Red, and Heartbreak Hotel Pink; perfume that displayed Elvis' picture on the label; Elvis record players and record boxes; Elvis photo albums and autograph books; and a clothing line, including black jeans with colorful stitching, scarves, T-shirts, hats, and even underwear—most sporting Elvis' name and titles of his biggest hits. All told, when the merchandizing program hit full speed, fifty products were being marketed through places like Sears, Montgomery Ward, Woolworths and others. *Variety* noted it was the "first all-out merchandising campaign in memory aimed at teens, not 'moppets.'"

To exploit Elvis' movies at the highest level, the Colonel insisted that he sing in every one of them; producing soundtracks that came out just prior to the movie release. People who saw the movies in theatres gobbled up the records like hungry bears. And the Colonel wolfed down more and more of Elvis' earnings, continuously finding creative ways to increase his share of the profits.

On the movie angle, the Colonel was fortunate to attract the attention of Hal Wallis. Wallis had happened on Elvis when he was performing on Dorsey's *Stage Show* and immediately saw the potential — this controversial young singer not only electrified live audiences, he also had the charisma to translate that allure onto a movie screen.

Wallis was not a newcomer to movie making, having launched his career in Hollywood in the 1920s, later producing some of Warner Brothers' best movies, including *Sergeant York* and *Casablanca*. In his Warner Brothers' days, he had worked with huge stars, luminaries like Humphrey Bogart, Ingrid Bergman, and Bette Davis. He was a maker of legends — just what Elvis needed.

Although new to the movie set, Elvis scoffed off the need for acting lessons, declaring, "I don't think you learn to become an actor, I think you just, maybe you've got a little bit of acting talent and develop it. If you learn to be an actor, in other words, if you're not a real actor — you're false." And, he bragged, he was good at memorizing, recalling his memorization of General MacArthur's farewell address and Lincoln's Gettysburg speech.

Elvis also packed another potent weapon that could shoot him into stardom. After watching Marlon Brando and Jimmy Dean, he discerned why young girls went for them, and he knew he had the same qualities. "We're sullen; we're broodin'; we're something of a menace. I don't understand it exactly, but that's what the girls like in men. I don't know anything about Hollywood, but I know you can't be sexy if you smile. You can't be a rebel if you grin."

Elvis understood the bad boy attraction.

He didn't need to smile or grin in his first movie, a story chronicling the lives of four brothers during the Civil War. Although Wallis had signed Elvis with Paramount, it wasn't an exclusive deal. So, when he heard about a movie that might be a good match for Elvis at Twentieth

# LOVE ME TENDER

Century Fox, he helped set up the opportunity for Elvis to co-star in *Reno Brothers*, with filming starting in August, 1956, which fit into both Elvis' and the Colonel's need to get Elvis off the road. In his secondary role, Elvis played the youngest Reno brother, Clint, who stayed at home to help on the farm while his older brothers went to war. When the family got word that the oldest son, Vance, had been killed, Clint married his older brother's sweetheart, but it turns out that Vance wasn't killed. The family splinters when he returns home out of the blue. Before the drama ends, Clint (Elvis) is shot and dies.

Elvis was concerned about his fans seeing him die on the screen, but he went along with the script, memorizing not only his parts but also everyone else's. He was ready and raring to go, as a hillbilly might say. The movie had three songs, but he was willing to accept that, thinking he could get to straight drama in his next movie. Scotty and Bill were glad about the singing, since they had been offered a tryout to be back-up musicians. It didn't work out though, because the musical director didn't think they were quite "hillbilly" enough. Although not surprised the Colonel didn't take up for them — he never did and would have fired them long ago if Elvis had allowed it —, they were dumbfounded when Elvis merely said that maybe he could work it out for them to be in his next movie. Already aggravated at the Colonel because he had moved them from a percentage of the take to a straight salary, Scotty and Bill were furious. They had been with Elvis since the beginning, and it simply wasn't right. They knew he was "the" star, but they had tutored him on the road and had even brought their own brand of excitement to his shows. Bill, a ham, had been particularly good at keeping the crowds stirred up.

But it didn't matter. The shooting of the film, now re-titled *Love Me Tender*, started without Bill and Scotty. The theme song, a rewrite of an old Civil War song called "Aura Lee," was a ballad. Some concern existed among those who had never heard Elvis sing anything except rock 'n' roll that he could handle a love song. The naysayers were stunned at the simplicity and beauty Elvis brought to the song as he stood as still as a statue in front of a stained glass window, the words flowing from his lips like sweet nectar. Elvis was amused. "People think all I can do is belt," he told a Hollywood writer. "I used to sing nothing

63

but ballads before I went professional. I love ballads." He added he had even decided to start using a few ballads on his tours.

It didn't take Elvis long to find that making films could be as strenuous as being on the road. Up at 5:30, he worked without stopping, often until late in the day. He gave the same 150 percent to acting he had given to singing, recalling later that he fell asleep talking to June on the phone several times. His work ethic earned him points on the set, and his sincere desire to learn from the other actors and the director impressed his co-stars, who were so charmed they went out of their way to help the fledgling actor.

While shooting *Love Me Tender*, Elvis took time to cut some songs for a record to fulfill his RCA obligations. Once again, he was in charge, recording, playing back, and repeating the sequence over and over until he felt good about a song. Bones Howe said it was like he was waiting for the magic to appear in a song, but that only happened when the other musicians felt what he felt—the same energy and excitement. One of the best songs of the session was "Old Shep," the story of a boy and his dog, and in an unusual moment, Elvis insisted he wanted to play the piano on this song. Several other songs were cut, including "Too Much," "Anyplace Is Paradise," and "When My Blue Moon Turns to Gold Again." But Elvis couldn't get away from "Love Me Tender," coming back to it repeatedly.

Back on the set, Elvis became increasingly comfortable. And, he was beginning to like living in Hollywood, sometimes taking over the whole floor of a hotel. He had to move fairly often, since his fans ran amok whenever they found where he was hiding out. Even some of his own family and friends, who followed him like puppy dogs wherever he went, became rowdy, so it wasn't long before he had to find a house. Hotels were just too stiff-necked for Elvis' brand of fun.

In early September, Elvis interrupted filming—for his first appearance on the *Ed Sullivan Show*. Despite Sullivan's efforts to tame him, Elvis generated his typical girl-frenzying performance, even if it was with shrugs and tongue probes instead of gyrating hips. The crowd froze when, for the first time in public, he sang "Love Me Tender," enthralled at hearing their king sing a gentle love ballad. Instead of screams, fans in the audience almost whimpered, and their stifled emotional cries stirred him as much as their screams. Of course, when Elvis broke into Little Richard's "Ready Teddy," followed by "Hound Dog," the fans went wild again, unleashing their animal-like screeches, sounds from the heat of the earth.

More than 80 percent of the households in America who had televisions watched the *Sullivan* show that night. And it wasn't Sullivan who attracted them. In their living rooms, fans knelt at the feet of their king, oblivious to the host who had tried to subdue their idol.

Surreptitiously, a few disc jockeys managed to tape the performance of "Love Me Tender" and started playing it on air. Overnight pre-release orders for the record approached the million mark. The movie hadn't even been wrapped up, and its theme song was a hit. No one ever doubted again that Elvis could capture hearts with songs of love.

After returning to Hollywood to wind up filming, Elvis flew to Memphis and then within a few days drove to Tupelo for a grand homecoming. Tupelo had rolled out the red carpet for their hometown hero, proud he was coming "home." It was a triumphal march back to the city where Elvis and his parents had left only a few short years ago with everything they owned piled in and on top of their car, or as country folk might say, "without a pot to pee in." That was yesterday. Today, Elvis had more money, in another Southern saying, than "Carter had liver pills." After a huge parade along streets with banners welcoming Elvis home, he joked with friends after he entered the fairgrounds about having to climb the fence to get in when he was a kid, often being escorted out after being caught.

Mr. and Mrs. Presley reveled in the moment, dressed like proud peacocks to show their old friends how far they had come—on Elvis' unfettered generosity. "The boy is really taking care of us," Vernon told one person, less than three years after telling Elvis not to quit his job. Sadness overtook Gladys, though, as she recalled how poor they had been, and then she became frightened when her son's vocal cords turned the crowd of fifty thousand into raving maniacs. Forty law officers held the crowd at bay, but it was so ribald that at one point Elvis stopped and asked the crowd to calm down so little kids wouldn't get hurt.

Elvis had thought the filming was finished before he left for Tupelo, but as it turned out, he had to fly back to Hollywood for a few more takes. Then it was on the road again, this time to Texas, where the *Dallas Morning News* reported a hysterical crowd of 26,500 swung out of control when Elvis started singing. Once again, the band had to go on instinct—or at least Elvis' moves as seen from the rear—since they couldn't hear anything. D. J. Fontana remembers thinking it looked like a war zone.

Although worried about the riots, the Colonel was basking in the afterglow of the "Love Me Tender" single. It was on the way up the *Billboard* charts, having already been certified as a gold record. The old carny didn't even notice that his star was struggling, getting only four hours of sleep a night. And Elvis couldn't go anywhere without being mobbed. The only peace he got was when he holed up in a hotel or at home in Memphis. Even so, Elvis wouldn't have slowed down even if the Colonel had suggested it. "The Lord can give and the Lord can take away. I might be herding sheep next year," he once said. Gladys was more worried about Elvis getting mugged, even killed. She just couldn't seem to rest easy, fretting night and day about her baby.

Back in Tennessee, Elvis divided his time between Barbara and June, whom Elvis had invited to Memphis for a visit. When June read about Elvis and Barbara being mobbed on a date, she knew her time with Elvis was drawing to a close. He belonged to his fans, and no one girl could hold him. June reached the end of her rope when she heard Natalie Wood was coming to visit Elvis while she was still with him in Memphis. Enough was enough. She packed her bags and went home to Biloxi.

Elvis went back to the *Ed Sullivan Show*. Having declared on television that Elvis was a "real decent, fine boy" and that he had "never had a pleasanter experience on our show with a big name than we've had with you," Sullivan wanted to bring back the young man who had boosted his ratings into the galaxy. This time a more confident and calmer Elvis appeared. Basking in his newfound big-screen stardom, he wanted to tone down his critics' condemnation.

The biographer Guralnick says not only was Elvis a recording star and a movie star, "he was a servant of the Lord and the master of his own destiny; for one brief moment there was not even a hint of imposture in his mind." Undoubtedly, this time Elvis came with a prepared message to the Big Apple: He was not a devil leading teenagers to perdition. In an interview with the *New York Times*, Elvis swayed reporters, telling them he wished he could talk personally with those who thought he was leading their youngsters astray. "Because I think I could change their minds and their viewpoint." He had examined his conscience, he declared, and asked himself if he was accidentally harming his fans. He had also consulted his Bible. "My Bible tells me that what he sows he will also reap, and if I'm sowing evil and wickedness it will catch up with me. I'm right sure of that, sir, and I don't think I'm bad for people. If I did think I was bad for people, I would go back to driving a truck, and I really mean this." He hooked the reporters and reeled them in. This young man was real, and he wasn't a pitchfork holding demon; he was a born-again Christian who cared about his admirers.

While he was trying to persuade the parents of teenagers that he meant—and did—no harm, some of his fans were protesting his death in *Love Me Tender*. Their efforts hit home with the movie's producers, and they filmed a new ending to the film, superimposing a very-much-alive-Elvis over the dying character he portrayed, singing the film's title song.

With that done, the Colonel announced a new RCA contract that guaranteed Elvis royalty payments of $1,000 per week for at least the next twenty years. Unbelievably, RCA had already sold ten million of Elvis' singles. That, plus road show tickets and guarantees, along with merchandise revenue, put Elvis over the million dollar mark in income. *Look* magazine revealed the true lovers in *Love Me Tender*: Colonel Tom Parker and Hank Saperstein—"two grown men who love him true and tender and hope that they will never have to let him go.

# 10
# SUSPICION

*Suspicion torments my heart. . .why torture me?*

~Doc Pomus

Elvis loved going to movies—he saw *Rebel Without a Cause* more than forty times and became a huge fan of its star, James Dean. When Dean died in a car accident in September 1955, movie producers had to find a replacement—someone as good-looking and sexy as Dean. Elvis fit the bill perfectly. Gaited, colorful, beautiful.

Elvis poured his heart and soul into *Love Me Tender*, or as critic Bosley Crowther wrote in the *New York Times* after the November 15, 1956, premier in New York, he went at it "as if it were *Gone With the Wind.*" Unfortunately, Elvis' co-stars didn't fare so well with Crowther, who said, "Richard Egan is virtually lethargic as the brother who comes home from war, and Debra Paget is bathed in melancholia."

For Elvis, the *Times* stood out as an exception to the movie reviews about his performance. Fearing the worse, he had fled to Las Vegas before the movie premiered, much like he hid out at the movie theater in Memphis the night his first record aired on the radio. While fifteen hundred teenagers lined up for the first show many miles away, Elvis tried to be incognito in Vegas, one of the few places where he could blend in with other celebrities.

With or without the presence of Elvis, critics had a field day. Some criticism stemmed from the awkwardness in having Elvis' character sing in the middle of scenes. Adding songs for the sole purpose of attracting his raving fans was deemed artificial. It wasn't as if the songs were built into the story—they were superfluous.

The *Reporter* attacked Elvis as "an obscene child" who was "excessively sorry for himself...a lone wolf who wants to belong." Undoubtedly the *Reporter* had picked up on Elvis' dream of becoming the next James Dean, carping about how Elvis "slouch[ed]" and "amble[d]," adding a denunciation of his music as nothing more than "a vacillation between a shout and a whine."

Some of the harshest criticism arose from the attempt to change the negative impression created in live performances — provocative movements seen as vulgar by the suspicious-minded parents. *Time* magazine was particularly disparaging in describing the "new" Elvis image, asking, "Is it sausage?"

Despite the negative reviews, when the film opened nationally a week later on the 21st, Paramount Studios had a hit on their hands. The studio made its largest release, sending 575 prints to theaters across the country, almost triple the normal release. And fans flocked to the film; it was second at the box office to the release of the posthumous release of *Giant* with Elvis' hero James Dean, plus top stars Elizabeth Taylor and Rock Hudson. Paramount made all of the cost of making the movie with weeks.

His Hollywood makeover aside, Elvis vacillated from embarrassment about his performance to resentment that his loyal fans missed his astral acting in their mania over his singing. His friend Clint Greaves related that Elvis groaned, "I'll never make it, it will never happen, because they're never going to hear me 'cause they're screaming all the time."

Though disillusioned and discouraged, Elvis refused to give up his dream of being a legitimate movie star. And he darn well wasn't going to take lessons despite what the critics said. He was going to do it *his* way. He had at least one review — from the *Los Angeles Times* — to back him up: "Elvis can act...the boy's real good, even when he isn't singing."

Before he could get back on the movie set to prove himself and the *Los Angeles Times* right, Elvis went home to Memphis. Natalie Wood joined him for a few days, and Elvis enjoyed showing her his roots — the Lauderdale Courts where he lived, his high school, Sun Records, and places where he used to hang out. Natalie was taken aback by the constant attention Elvis drew. People followed him everywhere, and they hung out near his house waiting for Elvis to come out and sign autographs. Natalie quickly decided she wouldn't want to live that way and didn't tarry long before heading back to Hollywood. She was there long enough, though, to be pictured in the Memphis newspaper with Elvis, and seeing the photos, June felt more and more that Elvis had drifted away from her. He wasn't a "real" person—he was a star who played with people's feelings for his own amusement.

Whether harsh words were spoken by a movie critic or a girlfriend, Elvis was tormented by suspicion that he wasn't real, that his career was a house of cards destined to eventually collapse. He didn't understand why any girl wouldn't "wait a little longer" for him. As the song goes, "true love is hard to find." And he had people pulling at him from all directions.

It wasn't just the Colonel or movie stars who tugged Elvis away from June—and later from other girlfriends. It was also the constant need to be surrounded by his old Memphis friends. First it was Rod Wilson, and when Rod joined the Marines, Cliff Greaves, in addition to some of Elvis' cousins who were always around and traveled with him most of the time. The more popular Elvis became, the more he couldn't escape the crowds, the more he insulated himself with people he had known and trusted. Adored and worshiped like a king, Elvis felt alone in the sea of his fans.

When Elvis retreated to Vegas to await the reviews on *Love Me Tender*, he met Dottie Harmony, the next girlfriend on the growing list. Characteristically, Elvis gave his whole heart—at least for the moment—to Dottie. She saw a mercurial Elvis—the same man who called his mother every night ripped her phone off the wall when he became incensed because she was talking to another man. But Elvis always bought her a new phone, Dottie told friends, so she knew he was sorry. Like his other girls, she knew she had to take what he dished out if she had any hope of being the last girl standing.

The local girls were getting tired of Hollywood and Vegas women invading their home territory; so when Dottie showed up in Memphis, they greeted her with banners reading, "Go home, Dottie Harmony." They had an ally; the Colonel tried to interfere with Dorothy, shutting her out, but Gladys let him know in a heartbeat that when "Doroty" was in Memphis, she was part of the family. Gladys was as predictable as Elvis—she took his girls under her wing, protecting and encouraging them, hoping that each one would be the one to mean so much to Elvis that he would slow down and live a more normal life.

The picture Dorothy paints of Elvis isn't the stereotypical fun-loving guy roaming around Memphis on his motorcycle or the star-studded performer being mobbed by his fans. She says they read the Bible every night—Elvis read aloud and then he and Dorothy discussed the readings. "He was very religious," she recalls, adding, "There was nothing phony about that at all." But he was loyal to his fans and religiously went outside at the same time each evening to sign autographs. Elvis loved God and Elvis loved his fans, and he devoted time to both. Without them, he was nothing; they made him a star.

Despite the innocuous portrait of their time together drawn by Dorothy, June was livid when she saw pictures of Elvis and Dorothy enjoying Christmas together. That was worse than the time he spent with Natalie. It was Christmas, after all, and she had hoped to spend the holiday with him—or at least hear from him. Belatedly, she accepted that to Elvis relationships were a game, and "it really broke my heart." Knowing the situation was without hope, June soon found another man and didn't look back.

When he wasn't looking for new women, dealing with old ones, or giving one the grand tour in Memphis, Elvis spent the days before filming his next movie visiting old friends. One day he stopped by to see Sam Phillips and was introduced to a new piano player for whom Sam had just released a record. It wasn't long before Elvis and Jerry Lee Lewis were jamming with Carl Perkins and his brothers. Then Johnny Cash dropped by with his wife and joined them for a while. The astute Sam had his recorder on and captured the spontaneous jamming. It just so happened that a Memphis *Press-Scimitar* reporter was there, and the next day when he wrote about the session, he made the mistake of saying if Sam had been on his toes, he would have caught the session on tape. By the time the newspaper hit the streets, Sam wasn't only on his toes, he was one step ahead. He had hand-delivered copies of the recording to area DJs before the paper hit the streets. Of course, Sam told everyone the microphone had been on by accident. Still, he said, "...it was kind of like coming from the same womb" hearing the motley crew of stars and would-be stars fooling around together. Since it might never happen again, Sam was glad he had inadvertently caught it on tape. And Elvis was glad he could be himself with kindred music spirits. For once, no one suspected him of anything beyond the fun he was having.

# MY WAY

The Colonel wasn't too pleased with Sam's coup d'état, but he didn't have time to waste on the man who had given him the goose that laid the golden egg. To keep the goose laying, he needed to keep movies coming out. That was the only way to put some space between Elvis and his rabid fans and thus calm the critics calling him a demon. As Guralnick describes the controversy surrounding the star, Elvis was on a merry-go-round and couldn't get off without help from the Colonel and Hal Wallis. "Denounced from the pulpit, derided in the press, increasingly linked to the race issue. . .[Elvis'] music was being used to stigmatize a generation." Elvis had even been the subject of congressional hearings, Guralnick wrote.

At the beginning, the Colonel (and Elvis) had reveled in the huge crowds and screaming girls, but it was about to harm the "business." Hal Wallis, who had a reputation for polishing images and leading singers from the stage to the movie set with success, became the Colonel's "partner in crime," that is, make as much money as possible on Elvis. Granted, Wallis wasn't crass like the Colonel, and he had a sincere desire to help Elvis make his career long and profitable, but his professionalism aside, he still wanted to make money. Even so, he was canny enough to be cautious of the Colonel, once saying, "I'd rather try and close a deal with the Devil."

*Loving You* was the next vehicle to distance Elvis from the mania and direct him toward the safety of the big screen. Behind him, Elvis was leaving a trail of women asking, as "Suspicion" does, "Do you speak the same words to someone else when I'm not there?"

# 11
# ALL THAT I AM

*All that I am or ever hope to be*

*Lies in your hands*

~Roy C. Bennett and Sid Tepper

Over the next 20 months following the release of *Love Me Tender,* Elvis starred in three more films: *Loving You, Jailhouse Rock,* and *King Creole.* Of those, *Jailhouse Rock* and *Loving You* were two of Elvis' top five grossing movies, with *Jailhouse Rock* bringing in more than $30 million (about $237 million in 2011) and *Loving You* approaching $29 million (almost $230 million today).

Unlike *Love Me Tender,* all three of the other movies completed before Elvis entered the Army in 1958 had bits and pieces of his life story, altered but not artfully camouflaged, with a starring role developed especially for him. What all four movies had in common was the addition of songs to exploit the adulation of fans.

Hal Wallis knew how to capitalize on Elvis' appeal, and that was by creating a "vehicle," defined by Doll as a film designed almost unambiguously around the image of a particular star, overshadowing plot and character development. She also notes that the use of Elvis iconography—personal traits, background, and appearance that fans associated with him because of publicity and public performances— allowed a movie to capitalize on the connection fans drew between the leading character of the movie and the real Elvis. Fans flocked to the movies to see the "authentic" Elvis—the same one they viewed on television and saw at concerts. He might have a different name, but the hair and sideburns were visible, the colorful clothing was present (as was his often-copied turned-up collar), and Elvis' fondness for Cadillacs always appeared.

In addition to the iconographic features, the use of Scotty Moore, D.J. Fontana, and Bill Black as back-up musicians in all but the first of

Elvis' early movies added another known factor, making the connection to Elvis even more realistic. And, of course, the enviable, or to his critics not so enviable, gyrations from Elvis' live performances were on display, although Elvis did have to contain the range of his movements because of the cameras.

The three films also all featured an against-all-odds success theme — a gifted musician with a new approach suffers from malicious attacks as he battles his way to the top. Portraying Elvis this way illustrated that he wasn't a lone wolf — that other change-agent musicians faced similar criticism because they threatened the status quo. In other words, Doll says, the success theme — rags to riches despite mean critics — helped people realize Elvis wasn't dangerous — and he wasn't unique in the way he held sway over a new generation and its fondness for a different style of music.

Wallis and Parker wanted to use the films to depict all that Elvis was or ever hoped to be in a favorable light, while shaping opinion that Elvis wasn't as different or devilish as some alleged.

In *Loving You*, Elvis played a young Southern singer (Deke Rivers) who mirrored Elvis' rise to fame, his ability to set young girls on fire, and the accusations that he was the damnation of teenagers. Deke, like Elvis, played with a country band but also had an affinity for R&B. From his mannerisms to messages written with lipstick on a Cadillac, elements were drawn from Elvis' life and woven into Deke's. Along with his troublemaker reputation for leading teenagers down a forbidden path, Deke even suffered sneers about his long sideburns. Echoing Elvis' real life strategy, the film had Deke appearing on television in an effort to counter his negative image.

Before the movie ends, Deke has morphed into Elvis, singing and shaking his hips, swaying his way into the hearts of Elvis' young fans. Gladys and Vernon even make an appearance as part of Deke's audience, and if the fans hadn't been sure it was Elvis' life story before the camera swings to the elder Presleys, they lost all doubt at that point. They bought Deke as a real-life Elvis hook, line, and sinker — even if his hair was coal-black, the only serious deviation from the real Elvis. That change had suited Elvis fine, since he believed dark-haired stars, such as Tony Curtis, were the most serious actors — and movie stars with dark hair seemed to have longer-running screen careers than lighter-haired men.

Elvis was pleased, too, that the music in *Loving You* fit the script better than the songs that had been incorporated into *Love Me Tender*. And, it picked up some of the same qualities — the sincere expression of inner joy and even a sense of spirituality — that Sam Phillips had envisioned in a singer. Ability to express such emotions came easily for Elvis, and he intuitively assumed the role of a man in turmoil. And as noted by biographer Guralnick, Elvis was able to achieve an almost subliminal stillness at his center that occasionally made its way to the surface, adding that these atypical times of feeling comfortable in his own skin on the movie set showed promise for Elvis as an actor. Those rare moments made Hal Wallis feel his intuition that a super star resided in Elvis wasn't the product of a hallucination.

While Elvis occasionally exhibited serenity within, peace was elusive — especially with Scotty and Bill. They increasingly felt relegated to the edge, often denied access to Elvis as they were pushed further and further away, almost insignificant in the larger group of musicians with whom Hal Wallis surrounded Elvis. Gladys and Vernon were able to avoid the fray and increasingly embraced Elvis' success. With movies, Elvis wasn't in danger of being mobbed. And, Elvis' parents were so proud of their beloved son they thought their hearts might burst. Elvis had climbed from the valley to the mountaintop and had arrived in grand style.

Vernon and Gladys went home before filming ended, and Elvis soon joined them, eager to see a house they had found that they thought would be perfect for the family. Called Graceland, it was a purchase Elvis never regretted. He was ecstatic he could give his parents such an elegant home.

After completing the purchase of Graceland, Elvis hit the road again. His first stop was Tupelo, where the Colonel, mindful of the continual need to polish Elvis' image, decided all profits from the concert would be donated to help build a youth recreation center for kids near Elvis' birthplace. Then the Colonel sent Elvis to Chicago to bring in some bucks. In his first show date, twelve thousand attended. Watching Elvis in his $2,500 gold-leaf suit, made specially for the tour, sent girls into spasms — thirteen of them fainted when Elvis appeared.

The Elvis entourage continued to grow, with George Klein and Arthur Hooten joining up partly because Elvis was tired of his cousin Junior, whose erratic behavior was becoming an embarrassment. It was on this tour, also, that Scotty, Bill, and D.J. began thinking about jumping ship. While Elvis pocketed millions, they were still on a $100 per week retainer that increased to $200 per week when they were working with Elvis. It didn't happen on this tour — ten cities in ten days — but a storm brewed on the horizon. For now, they would make the trek back to Hollywood with Elvis for filming his next movie. George, his cousin Gene Smith, and Arthur were going, too, and Cliff would be there waiting. The larger the party grew, the smaller the role played by the longtime back-up musicians. In an entourage of 15-20 friends and cousins, they felt on the fringe. It hurt that several of these guys were on the payroll, and they did nothing except "be there." Well, maybe they were always at Elvis' beck and call, but it was easy work for the money they were earning. Scotty and his fellow band members *were* pleased to notice they weren't the only ones who had to scatter when the Colonel appeared. Everyone knew to flap their wings and fly when the Colonel stuck his head in a room.

In Hollywood, *Jailhouse Rock* incorporated many of the same real-life similarities as *Loving You*: the sexual performing style, the core band members, the fondness for Cadillacs, the trademark turned-up collars and flashy clothes, and the iconic hair and sideburns all reflect the real-life Elvis. Vince Everett, the character Elvis plays, has his hair shorn in the movie, though, perhaps as a foreshadowing of Elvis' upcoming induction into the army.

The plot of *Jailhouse Rock* is a take-off on Elvis' rough, radical musician image. Playing a character named Vince Everett, Elvis' own life is only tangentially tied to the story of the working-class rebel who ends up in jail following a conviction for manslaughter. Even so, the success story theme — the rise and transition of a country music singer to a rock 'n' roll star — carries the film. And, Doll notes that, like Elvis, Vince "radiates a sexuality that's instinctual, animalistic, and dangerous...."

Elvis had evolved into a pattern of movie making interspersed with live concerts — limited tours in big cities. Wherever he was, whatever he was doing, Elvis had the reputation of working his heart out. Part of his success emanated from his dedication and focus. And part of his fun came from new relationships — male friends and pretty girls.

His latest flame was a nineteen-year-old beauty-contest winner, Anita Wood. A West Tennessee girl, she and Elvis hit it off from the get-go. Anita came from Jackson, about 90 miles east of Memphis, so Elvis gave her the grand tour of "his" city, continuing the pattern of taking friends by his old home and other stomping grounds. He seemed to need periodic visits to his past — where he had come from — to reinforce that he never wanted to go back to the poverty-stricken life of his youth.

Sometimes he tried to shed his past, like when he had a falling out with Dewey Phillips, who had repeatedly embarrassed him in front of his Hollywood friends. In other situations, Elvis desperately needed to cling to his roots. When rumors made the rounds that he was prejudiced, Elvis was stunned. Accused of saying, "The only thing Negroes can do for me is buy my records and shine my shoes," Elvis knew his history would defend him: "I never said anything like that, and people who know me know I wouldn't have said it." But racial tension was tightly strung in Memphis in 1957. That year Laurie Sugarmon, who had graduated Phi Beta Kappa from Wellesley, and Maxine Smith, who held a degree from Middlebury, were denied admission to a graduate program at the school now known as the University of Memphis. Race was the sole criterion for denial — they were black and "blacks were, de facto, not acceptable."

With such racial injustice prevalent, reporters would have had a field day had they been able to stir up evidence Elvis looked down on blacks. Instead, all they found were men who stood up for him. Dr. W. A. Zuber, a black Tupelo doctor, told a reporter from *Jet* magazine Elvis had often spent time with black quartets and that he had attended "Negro 'sanctified' meetings." From pianist Dudley Brooks, the reporter heard that Elvis "faces everybody as a man." Ivory Joe Hunter, who had been invited to Elvis' home, declared, "Elvis showed me every courtesy, and I think he's one of the greatest." With several other testimonies, *Jet* soon concluded, "To Elvis, people are people, regardless of race, color or creed."

If only the devil-inspired reputation had been as easy to shed.

But it was not to be. As long as the near-riots continued when Elvis teased crowds with his suggestive dancing and writhing, the devil-mongers continued their venom. Although he repeatedly maintained that being "limp as a rag" came as easily singing gospel hymns as rock 'n' roll, his detractors had to do no more than point to his explosive "Hound Dog" rendition, which had become Elvis' personal national anthem. In Vancouver, when the Canadian Mounties couldn't hold back the crowd, the Colonel had to rush onstage and pull Elvis out of the reach of the teenagers overrunning the stage. Before the night ended, the stage had been overturned, George Klein recalls, "with kids grabbing music stands, instruments, drumsticks, everything they could get. That was a pretty scary night."

The press was again ruthless, with the *Vancouver Province* declaring Elvis' performance was nothing more than "subsidized sex." The paper added that the performance "had not even the quality of a true obscenity; merely an artificial and unhealthy exploitation of the enthusiasm of youth's body and mind." After Vancouver, Elvis was relieved to get back in a recording studio. He loved his fans, recognizing, "All that I am, I am because of you," but a little distance gave him breathing room.

Scotty and Bill were glad to get off the road, too, because they had been promised their own recording time after Elvis finished his session at the RCA studio. As it turned out, Elvis went too long, following his typical pattern of recording, play back, recording, over and over until it sounded "his way." Let down that the promise they could record had been broken, they sent, along with D.J., a letter of resignation to Elvis. Enough was enough. They were tired of playing second and third fiddle. It was time to move on.

Although Elvis later offered a raise if they would come back, the split only widened when Bill and Scotty poured their hearts out to a local newspaper. They claimed Elvis had promised the more he made the more they would make but had gone back on his word. It was the Colonel who had cut the musicians out of their take, but they vented about Elvis. He could have taken up for them if he had cared. But the pull of Elvis was difficult to resist, and several weeks later, Scotty, Bill, and D.J. ate humble pie. Though they came back on board, with all the bad feelings aired publicly, the relationships were never again the same.

Elvis, a prisoner of his celebrity status, felt embattled. It wasn't enough that his own musicians had betrayed him. He had to endure constant criticism from all directions. When Frank Sinatra was quoted in a magazine article attacking rock 'n' roll as "phony and false," Elvis went on the defensive. He couldn't let Sinatra's allegation that rock 'n' roll "was sung, played, and written for the most part by cretinous goons and by means of its almost imbecile reiteration, and sly, lewd, in plain fact, dirty lyrics" go unchallenged. In effect, when Sinatra proclaimed, "The genre manages to be the martial music of every side-burned delinquent on the face of the earth," Elvis took it personally. Even so, his response was tempered, beginning with recognition that Sinatra had a right to say whatever he pleased, even acknowledging Sinatra's stature in the world of music and drama. But his message was clear: "He's mistaken about this. This is a trend, just the same as he faced when he started years ago," ending with, "You can't knock success."

Despite Elvis' even-handedness, his performance that night before a crowd of 9,000 screaming fans brought more bad press. The *Los Angeles Mirror* asserted if any more proof had been needed that Elvis was nothing more than a sex show "it was proved last night." The writer of that assessment, Dick Williams, added that Elvis' performance reminded him of "one of those screeching, uninhibited party rallies which the Nazis used to hold for Hitler." Perhaps the most insulting report was a statement describing Elvis' music as "a terrible popular twist on darkest Africa's fertility tom-tom displays."

Elvis toned down his next concert, and no one cried foul about the censorship except Yul Brynner. The king generated swoons and screams if he did no more than wiggle his little finger. And, as long as Elvis was making nearly two million dollars a film (more than $15 million in 2011), the Colonel's share was enough to keep him off Elvis' back most of the time. After a quick tour in Hawaii where the crowds played out their adoring fanatics' role, Elvis seemed glad to head back to Memphis and his new home. In calmer moments, he remembered that all he had become had started with his parents. They were "[his] heart, [his] soul, and his dream come true." His fans made it possible for him to show his appreciation and love through setting them up in Graceland.

# 12

# MANSION ON THE HILLTOP

*I want a mansion, a harp, and a crown*

~Ira Stanphill

Elvis' parents (and Elvis himself when he was in Memphis) had been living contentedly in a home he had bought them on Audubon, but neighbors had begun complaining about the incessant hordes of young people hanging around and had even filed a lawsuit against the family, alleging they were creating a public nuisance. The Presleys themselves were tolerant of the fans, even those who picked blades of grass from their yard as souvenirs. Elvis had made it clear he wouldn't be where he was without his fans, and he didn't want them driven away by police. So Gladys and Vernon had begun looking around for a house that would provide more privacy. Just after they returned from visiting Elvis in California, Gladys discovered the perfect place.

Elvis adored his mother, and a large portion of the joy from his success sprang from being able to make her happy. When she called him in Los Angeles to say she and Vernon had found a house with acreage they thought he would like, he promised he would look at it as soon as he was back in Memphis. Just as he had bought her the pink and white Crown Vic (even though she didn't know how to drive) with some of his first "real" money, he didn't hesitate to pay the asking price of $102,500 ($785,000 in 2011) for the estate she fancied. That the Southern mansion provided him with the ultimate symbol of success was a side benefit but one he treasured. For Elvis, as Keogh notes, it was like having his own Tara, especially since Graceland had been built in the same year *Gone with the Wind* was released. And, one can imagine Gladys saying to herself, "You've come a long way, baby," as she compared her new home to the two-room shotgun house she had once been so proud to call home.

Although Elvis made over a million dollars in 1958, he did not pay cash for the house. After a trade-in of $55,000 for the old house he had

80

bought his parents, he paid $10,000 in cash and financed the remainder. If the Colonel hadn't nixed a lucrative deal with a bubblegum manufacturer who wanted to strip newly installed paneling from the house on Audubon, cut it up, and put it as prizes in packages of bubblegum, Elvis might have been able to pay cash. At first this seems surprising, out of character for the Colonel, but beneath his decision was a devious desire not to conflict with his own merchandising deals.

Vernon would have haggled over the price for the house, but Elvis didn't bother. What mama wanted, mama got, and the price was irrelevant. She had cared for him in the two-room shotgun house where he had been born, and now he would take care of her in the most beautiful house he could find. He wanted something that would not only equal, but also surpass, the five-acre Bel Air estate owned by Red Skelton. Like Skelton, he needed a multi-car garage (Skeleton had room for 11 while Elvis could park 20). Elvis had been impressed at the way the wealthy comedian had mixed high brow and low brow—his 35,000-gallon swimming pool was graced with a life-size stuffed gorilla in the nearby shower room—and he wanted to create something similar; distinctive and unusual, yet tasteful. Skelton and Elvis also shared a deep appreciation for how far they had come—a sad tramp doll in his living room was a constant reminder for Skelton, and at Graceland, Elvis ate peanut butter and banana sandwiches to stay grounded. Intriguingly, Keogh also points out that both Elvis and Skelton had undercurrents of sadness beneath their public personas. The trappings of wealth weren't enough to satisfy their soul yearnings. Regardless, for both men, an extravagant home was an outward sign of success, though their inner thirst remained unquenched.

With all his work in Hollywood, Elvis had considered buying a house in California near other big stars, but he was at heart a Southern boy, and there his roots would remain. Besides, on the grounds of a Tennessee mansion, his mama could have a chicken coop so she could watch her hens outside her kitchen window. The Hollywood types might not appreciate the clucking chickens or a crowing rooster at daybreak, but Gladys did—she never lost her love of the simple life, although she appreciated what wealth had brought her family. She could dress up when she had to for important events, but in Memphis, secluded on the 18.25-acre estate, she could wear housedresses, living the good life in country fashion.

Graceland had been built about eight miles south of downtown Memphis by Dr. and Mrs. Thomas D. Moore in 1939. Although today it seems small by comparison to large-scale mansions, at the time the 18-room home had the feel of Southern gentility. The Moores had named their estate in honor of the Mrs. Moore's Aunt Grace, who had given them the property, and Elvis chose not to change the name, remarking that amazing grace had made it possible for him to buy the house.

Described by the Memphis *Commercial Appeal* as a palatial home with Corinthian columns designed in the Georgian colonial style, the house sits at the top of a small rise. Clad with Mississippi fieldstone, it stands out against a backdrop of silvery green trees. "As you roll up the drive, you sense [Graceland's] fine heritage from the past in its general feeling of aristocratic kindliness and tranquility," the article noted; adding "an air of subtle luxury...pervades the exterior [and] seeps through the walls and penetrates every room in the house...." Towering oaks added the final touch, proudly shading the drive, which would lead to the only privacy Elvis would know in the coming years—and then only because he added a rock wall and gates with a music motif to keep fans at bay. (The notes on the gates represent the first few bars of "Love Me Tender.")

From the beginning, Elvis determined his house would be grander than Skelton's. The most important change would be to create the most beautiful bedroom in Memphis for his mother. And he wanted a working soda fountain, where he and his friends could lounge and drink ice cream sodas and Cokes.

Although Elvis' tastes in decorating were as definitive and vibrant as his notable fashion choices, he didn't personally have time to supervise turning the house into his castle. Sam Phillips had recently engaged a man named George Golden to decorate his own new home, and because Elvis liked the flamboyant result, he hired Golden to re-do Graceland.

Golden's creative talent had taken him from selling Lipton iced tea to retrofitting several flatbed trucks with illuminated miniature rooms, built to scale—with everything from carpet and wallpaper to a two-foot sofa in chartreuse satin. He attracted clients by driving around Memphis, showcasing the rooms. After consultation, most of his clients had him present sketches, but Elvis had no time for that. He knew what he wanted, and he wanted it done quickly. In addition to the special bedroom for his mother, he wanted an entrance hall with a ceiling that would look like a night sky lit by stars. As if he could see the room in his mind, he dictated a white, 15-foot custom-built sofa for the living room, a gigantic coffee table, black consoles, and elegant shades on tall lamps, flecked with gold. No antiques anywhere—contemporary furniture wouldn't remind him of his poverty-stricken past; and antique furniture meant nothing to him—it was merely old, and he had had enough of cast-off pieces in his early life.

Elvis specified purple walls with gold trim for the living room and dining room, but after he left for California, his mother quietly overruled that choice, replacing it with a deep, yet soft, blue.

For himself, Elvis wanted a monstrosity of a bed—eight feet square—painted black and trimmed in white leather. His bedroom walls would be dark, dark blue, with a mirror covering one whole wall.

And he wanted a swimming pool, surrounded by a sunken patio with a six-foot pink stone wall. Cost was not a factor, and the decorating likely equaled the price of the house. The bottom line was he wanted an exciting home. Like the king's singing, his castle would be done his way. "You're here, make a damn statement," he said. From the peacocks in the stained glass windows between the living room and the music room holding his grand piano to the live peacocks that sashayed up and down the driveway, Elvis' home made a huge statement: He had arrived, not with pride or bravado, but with a sense that as a family they had traveled a rough road, and together they had made it to this point. (The peacocks made their own statement—they pecked the finish off his black Rolls-Royce.)

Just as his flashy clothes engendered criticism, the ostentatious decorating, including the "jungle room," aroused criticism from those who thought the trappings of wealth should reflect sophistication and class. To many, Elvis had taken the stately mansion and turned it into an embarrassment to Memphis' upper crust. Ever sensitive to criticism of his music, his family and friends, and his lifestyle, Elvis harbored self-doubt about his home. His doubts so troubled him that at the time of his mother's death, he said to the wife of his dentist, "Mrs. Hofman. I don't know if this is the right time, but the newspapers have made my house sound so laughable, I would love to have your opinion of my home."

Obligingly, Mrs. Hofman went through his home, dragging along her husband, who noted at one point that the modern sculpture above the fireplace was the same "Rhythm" he had in his dental office. After the tour, Elvis haltingly asked what she thought, wanting Mrs. Hofman's opinion but fearful it would corroborate critics' derision of his tastes. Without hesitating, Mrs. Hofman told him, "If you give me the key, I'll swap with you." She provided the perfect answer to reassure the shaky man who needed validation. Others might call his home laughable, but it was his home and it passed muster.

For Elvis, Graceland was more than grace personified; it was, as Keogh described, his "mansion over the hilltop." She suggests "Graceland was...the physical manifestation of all that Elvis had accomplished" in the same way that Carnegie, Rockefeller, Jay Gould, and J.P. Morgan had expressed their success through "gilded Newport 'cottages' and sprawling Fifth Avenue domiciles." More importantly to Elvis, Graceland was God's stamp of approval. If God hadn't been with him, he wouldn't have been successful. Without God in his corner, Graceland would have been an impossible dream.

Although he was away for weeks and even months at a time on the road, in Hollywood, or on location filming, Graceland became home for Elvis. Even after his mother's death several years later, it was the place where he always found respite. There, life followed his nocturnal habits. Talk and sing until the sun began to rise in the sleepy sky, stay in bed until 4 p.m., and rise to start another day (really, another night). Elvis found privacy from the world in the late dark hours when he could rent whole movie theatres, fairgrounds, roller rinks or other venues for his personal enjoyment, protected from clamoring fans. But when he was at home, he wanted his mama's kind of cooking—fried chicken, well-done steak, or meatloaf (which he once ate every day for eight months), accompanied by mashed potatoes doused in gravy—served on *his* schedule. Dinner was often at 2 a.m. since the first meal of the day (a hardy breakfast full of saturated fat) was usually dished up around 4 p.m.

Huge meals were the norm at Graceland, as were Elvis' antics. From mowing down his mother's tulips one day when he was horsing around on a riding lawnmower to the time he bought geese because he had heard they would keep grass down, there weren't many dull moments. The geese story was typical—Elvis bought them in Mississippi and hauled them to Memphis in the back seat of his car. Needless to say, the car was a mess by the time he arrived home. The much later time when Vernon's new wife attempted to redecorate Graceland while Elvis was away trumps all of the stories—when he returned he put her and all her belongings on the front lawn of Graceland in no time flat.

Lisa Marie has her own memories of times at Graceland with her father. In an interview with *Life* magazine in 1988, she recalled her dad "was always up to something, shooting off firecrackers or guns, running around driving golf carts or snowmobiles" (almost always minus snow since the white fluffy stuff was a rare occurrence in Memphis). Laughing, she says, "He'd pull me in a sled and scare me to death. On that long steep driveway that goes up to Graceland, he'd be pulling me up and falling at the same time." She adds he never called her Lisa unless he was mad—his favorite names were Button Head or Yisa.

When the king was in his castle, every evening around 6 or 7 o'clock he strolled down to the front gates to sign autographs for adoring fans. Today is no different—over 600,000 people visit Graceland every year—except the king is not present. When Elvis was there, it was the symbol of his success. Today it is the closest experience to Elvis a fan can have. For many, going to Graceland fulfills a lifelong dream. To walk through the halls where he walked, to glimpse the piano where he played gospel songs, and to see the kitchen where his mama and later his grandmother cooked his favorite meals are experiences that bring the king to a personal level.

Priscilla and Lisa Marie have ensured the home remains open to Elvis' devoted followers, and they have maintained the home as close to its original state as possible. Every ten minutes or so, buses drive up the hill and drop off visitors eager to walk through the rooms where Elvis lived. With cameras in hand, they come prepared to record their visit to share with friends or relive as they look at the pictures over the years.

Outside, two white wrought-iron benches, sitting beside regal lions, frame the walk to the steps beneath the columns. To the side of the front door, brilliant pink azaleas create a warm, welcoming entrance, and one can imagine Elvis' looking down on them in approval of the vibrant choice of color.

Graceland retains the look Elvis originally envisioned, the living room, dining room, and music room are decorated with elegant furniture, including a gilt-edge sofa and chairs covered with a white, silky fabric. Tasteful window treatments beside arched, built-in shelves and crystal chandeliers form the perfect backdrop for the dining room, where a table is set with crystal and china, accented with silver serving pieces. In the hall, an impressive oil painting of Elvis hangs, and beneath it a splash of blushing pink flowers reveals another Elvis touch.

As in the dining room, the carpet and walls in the living room are white, starkly contrasted against the royal blue draperies and the mostly royal blue crystal decorations atop a long dark glass table. On the mirrored shelves that surround the white and gray marble fireplace sit a bust of David and other statues; and a portrait of Elvis, as one does in most of the rooms, graces a wall.

Leaded glass windows with a peacock motif separate the living room and the music room. Elvis chose the flamboyant birds for their ancient symbolism of eternal life, resurrection, and rejuvenation.

The music room, converted from a sunroom, has had several baby grand pianos over the years, the longest lasting one a white and gold baby grand that was eventually replaced by the current black Story and Clark. This exquisite piano stands out among the gold in other parts of the room, including a mass of golden drapes covering the large windows that coordinate with a small gilded sofa. Again, as in many of the rooms, a television is present.

Upstairs, which is not open to the public, holds the mansion's bedrooms except the one where Gladys and Vernon slept. Blue velvet drapes at the top of the graceful, white-carpeted stairs block the entrance to Elvis' legendary bedroom, where he entertained his various women.

Gladys and Vernon slept in a tastefully furnished bedroom. The off-white furniture on white carpet contrasts richly with the bedspread made of velvet so deep in color it is difficult to discern whether it is blue or purple. It is easy to picture Gladys in her quiet room where she often sank to her knees in prayer for her son's safety.

When they were installed, the kitchen's harvest gold and avocado appliances were stylish and modern. The dark wood cabinets and a two-tiered counter create the effect of a cozy bar in the kitchen where Elvis and his gang hung out on the upholstered stools lining the counter. Sitting on the stove is a cast iron skillet, waiting for Minnie (Elvis' grandmother) to burn some bacon for Elvis.

The television room is clearly where Elvis retreated and reflects his touch with the sunny yellow soda fountain, three televisions (an idea he picked up from President Lyndon Johnson), and a stereo with his large selection of records to play on the turntable. This room was redecorated in 1974 to include mirrors on the wall and a mirrored bar incorporated into the soda fountain area. Black and gold graphics on the wall provide the backdrop for Elvis' trademark symbol — a TCB lightning bolt (Taking care of business — in a flash!). Priscilla helped Elvis design this special logo — an adaption of an expression commonly used in the black community.

One of the showiest parts of the house is across the hall from the television room, where the poolroom brandishes an unusual (some say garish) billowing of patchwork fabric covering the walls and the ceiling. More than 400 yards of fabric were used to decorate the dark room, including fabric draped in folds above the pool table, creating a tent effect above the stained glass pendant pool light. With a sofa in the same fabric as the walls and ceiling, the room feels like a cozy fox den, a good place to hide out and have some fun.

Contrary to expectations, the jungle room (which Elvis called his den) isn't overly animalistic, even though it does contain several monkey figurines. The story behind the room: Watching television one night, Elvis had seen a commercial for Donald's, a Memphis furniture store. In his perennial impetuous fashion, he jumped in his car and drove down to check out the furniture. In about half an hour, he had selected the furniture he needed to fill his Jungle Room and had the massive furniture with its fake fur upholstery delivered that same night.

At the entrance of the Jungle Room, a built-in bench with black fur fabric sits atop lush green carpet. Some of the chairs have high backs resembling totem poles, while others have arms carved to depict mythic birds. (One wonders if the intent was to represent a phoenix because of its ability to rise from ashes.) At one end of the room, wood-carved stools topped with more fake fur upholstery sit in front of a small bar. At the other end, a stuffed teddy bear sits beside a small child-like guitar on another fake fur chair. Although Elvis' first guitar was traded in and then tossed into a garbage can, one can almost see Elvis walking into the room, cradling his old guitar and stroking the strings as he recalls the days when he sang for neighbors in the housing project.

Elvis loved the ambiance of the Tahitian-styled room, which welcomed him like a big, cuddly bear. St. Francis, the patron saint of animals, guards the sanctuary as he sits silently on a shelf on a massive brick wall where streams trickle down a glistening waterfall. If one listens quietly, it is easy to imagine Elvis sitting in this room, the tinkling sounds of water soothing and relaxing him after a hard day of recording in the studio.

Today a four-car garage and Elvis' racquetball court have been converted into exhibits that showcase the reason fans flock to Graceland. These exhibits, for most visitors, are more impressive than the house. No matter how well versed in Elvis' career, even knowing how many gold and platinum records Elvis earned, seeing them displayed, one after another, after another, is stunning. And, the display is updated continuously as the king's records continue to sell, more than three decades after his death. The true magnitude of his past and ongoing success displayed at Graceland is mind-boggling. Complementing the astounding number of award winning records are showcases of Elvis' performance costumes. Visitors get a real sense of the uniqueness of the star's image, and for those fortunate enough to have seen Elvis in action, the flamboyant outfits bring back memories of the man and his magnetism.

Graceland, Elvis' mansion on a hilltop, where he brought his family to live in the luxury his superstar status had enabled, became the refuge where Elvis the man could escape, for a time, the legend and spotlight. The man who loved his mama, the man who became infatuated with a 14-year-old girl, the man who never lost his insecurity despite his worldly success, the man whose generous heart made him vulnerable, the man whose faith lifted him up when he was down. Through it all, as long as Elvis had his mama, it was all right—she was his rock of Gibraltar. She kept him grounded and buttressed his faith. When she was gone, his internal compass sometimes spun out of control.

# 13
# AS LONG AS I HAVE YOU

*Let the stars fade and fall*

*And I won't care at all*

~Benjamin Weisman and Fred Wise

Ever the doting son, Elvis would have gladly given all the millions he made to his parents if that would make them happy. Vernon *was* content, occupied with maintaining Graceland and supervising Elvis' finances. But Gladys missed having Elvis around. The house, too large, never felt like a home. Her sister Lillian remembered that Gladys "never was satisfied after she moved out there [Graceland]." Although she still had chickens to watch out the kitchen window on the mansion grounds to remind her of the simple life she had enjoyed, she couldn't find peace. She almost never left the house unless she was traveling to meet Elvis in some city for a few days, choosing to become a captive on the estate she had been so pleased to find.

Her son's life transformed into an out-of-control merry-go-round, Gladys fretted night and day something would happen to Elvis. She once commented, "I hope I'm in the grave before he is, because I could never stand to see him dead before me." Worry consumed her, overriding any joy she might have felt from the material comforts Elvis so generously provided.

At Christmas in 1957, just after moving into the hilltop estate, Elvis became infected with his mother's melancholy, and a spiritual emptiness permeated him. Unable to leave his house without hoards of fans descending, Elvis began to feel like his mother—a prisoner in his castle. Bleakly, he confided to a friend, "I can't go get a hamburger, I can't go in some greasy joint, I can't go waterskiing or shopping...." Earlier in the year, he had confessed to the pastor at First Assembly that he was miserable, that all of his money and his so-called friends left him feeling lost and alone. And he had told a *Photoplay* magazine reporter he had difficulty absorbing what had happened to him. Still, he said, he knew that "whatever I become will be what God has chosen for me…no matter what I do, I don't forget about God. I feel He is watching every move I make. And in a way it's good for me." Even so, Elvis' quest for spiritual peace continued to elude him.

In hindsight, Gladys' foreboding and Elvis' spiritual malaise foreshadowed the future.

Adding to the family's despondency, Elvis got a call from the local draft board the week before Christmas. The Colonel's attempts to keep Elvis out of the draft had failed. Though Elvis felt he should serve, he was concerned about what a two-year absence—and the inevitable loss of his sideburns and long hair—would do to his career. He could have joined the Navy and been given a special "Elvis Presley Company" or the Air Force, where he could have been assigned to help recruiting centers, but Elvis decided he didn't want favored treatment and chose the Army. He did ask for and receive a 60-day deferment to film *King Creole* since the producer had already invested several hundred thousand dollars in pre-production.

After handing out Christmas gifts—including a red Isetta sports car to the Colonel—and celebrating his 23rd birthday in early January, Elvis headed back to California, along with his usual entourage of friends and cousins.

Converting *King Creole* into an Elvis vehicle took finesse. Based on the novel *A Stone for Danny Fisher* by Harold Robbins, the central character is a wanna-be boxer who lives in New York. To be a better fit for Elvis, the script was rewritten with New Orleans as the locale, and Danny's aspiration switched to singing. Though the story lacked depth, the dramatic black-and-white cinematography pulled together and tightly woven by veteran director Michael Curtiz is the reason *King Creole* is often considered Elvis' best film, Elvis biographer Doll says.

Following the Elvis formula, his iconographic signatures were integrated into the story and its main character. The aspiring Danny wore his long hair in a pomade to make the front fall down in his eyes; one of Danny's goals in life was to have a pink Cadillac; back-up musicians included the Blue Moon boys, as well as the Jordanaires; and, Danny's sensuality came through as hot and suggestive. These easily recognizable elements drew fans like a magnetic force.

*King Creole* is the last movie Elvis made before his enlistment. It was also the last time the show business success myth was at the heart of his movies—playing the role of a talented musician who triumphs over external and internal demons (critics who misrepresent his style and a personal struggle to find meaning in the midst of success) in rising above obstacles to become a super star.

Doll notes that although nothing about Elvis changed, his image was reshaped in the iconographic movies: "Remarkably, these films effectively recast Elvis Presley's life story and star image from that of an unrepentant, Southern-based rebel who seemed threatening to the norms of society to a paradigm of the show business success myth, which was much more familiar and acceptable to mainstream audiences." If asked, Elvis might have remarked his image was recast to what he genuinely was—all the hype about his vulgarity and intent to corrupt teenagers was a bunch of nonsense.

Elvis' first films remade him into a young man who would be welcomed into anyone's living room. His characters, Deke, Vince, and Danny, reached out to Elvis' youthful audience, but their onscreen persona contained little of the provocative visual imagery and movements that outraged the prudish. In addition to limiting Elvis' mobility to a specified camera range, controlled choreography reduced some of the sensuality, as well as the spontaneity. The goal: to make the star's singing style less suggestive and aggressive and thus acceptable.

*King Creole* culminated the trio of success myth movies, which served as the perfect vehicles to begin refashioning Elvis' image. And *King Creole* was the lasting image as Elvis entered a two-year cooling-off period in the Army—a newly constructed picture of the singer left to gel in the minds of Americans. The wild young man who had left fans "all shook up" had been domesticated.

By the time Elvis returned as a performer, rock 'n' roll would be an acceptable part of musical genre. As the lines from "As Long as I Have You" go, the Colonel and Elvis wanted to "think of the future and forget the past." Generational issues would always exist, but soon rock 'n' roll would no longer bear the sole blame for parental/teenage conflicts.

Although the Colonel initially tried to keep Elvis from being drafted, Elvis went willingly; ready to return a little service in exchange for what America had done for him. He didn't want any special consideration, either, although he was allowed to live off base (both during and after basic training when his family and several friends flew to Germany, where he rented a house for the whole crew) with the goal of keeping army barracks from being besieged by young girls.

Losing his hair was another matter—at least to Elvis' fans. To make the change less drastic, he had his locks shorn a little each week before the "real" haircut the Army would give him. Fifty-five reporters and photographers witnessed the induction haircut, and even though Elvis knew he was losing a piece of his image, he managed to joke about the hairs falling to the floor: "Hair today, gone tomorrow," he quipped.

Although his fans despaired at not seeing Elvis for two long years, Elvis embraced the separation from his fans, saying, "I look upon my reporting to the army this way: it'll be a relief. It won't be a snap, I know, but it'll give me a chance to unwind, to catch my breath." His meteoric rise to fame, only three-and-a-half years from his audition with Sam Phillips to his Christmas draft notice, and the roller coaster highs and lows of popularity and criticism had taken their toll on the young idol. Sometimes he felt like an island in a sea of clamoring fans; other times he relished their attention and wanted to give as much of himself as possible. Still, the unrelenting hullabaloo was one part of Elvis' stardom he was glad to leave behind as he reported for induction into the Army.

Elvis spent the final ten days before he had to report to the Army in Memphis catching up with old friends, mending fences with some of them, including Dewey Phillips, saying goodbye to all the guys who had been his constant companions. He spent time with his family and with Anita, who had started her own climb to stardom. Elvis being Elvis, though, he didn't limit himself to one girl. One report had him entertaining hordes of girls, up to 12 by one count. Elvis himself admitted, much, much later, "I screwed everything in sight. I'd be crazy to get married now. I like to play the field."

Soon all that was behind him (at least until he got settled in Germany). His shock of hair shorn, and like the thousands of other inductees, garbed in a drab green uniform, light years away from his usual glimmering peacock attire, Elvis boarded a bus to Fort Hood,

Texas. He was assigned to the Second Armored Division, the "Hell on Wheels" outfit, made famous by another maverick, General George Patton.

Elvis tried to be a regular soldier, to be just one of the guys, even willingly pulling KP duty. Still, his fellow soldiers rode him hard when his homesickness became noticeable, making comments like, "Miss your teddy bears, Elvis?" or "You ain't wiggling right, boy." But Elvis was no common trainee and his sergeant, noticing his distress, let him come to his home to make calls to his mother, who arrived soon thereafter with the rest of Presley family to be near their boy, living in a house just outside the basic training post. That helped, and Elvis set out to be the best soldier possible, winning his marksman medal with a carbine and a sharpshooter award with a pistol. He was even named acting assistant squad leader.

Elvis adjusted to Army life and became accepted because he simply did what everyone else did without asking for special treatment other than receiving permission to live with Gladys and Vernon in off-base housing. No one could question that Vernon and Gladys were his dependents; he gave them more money than he kept for himself.

Despite his willingness to serve and initial embracing of time away from the pressure of his fans, Elvis' basic insecurity fed his worries. "It's all over," he would groan, "They aren't going to know me when I get back."

He soon found that was the least of his worries. His mother became ill while visiting him in Texas and had to return to Memphis, where she was admitted to the hospital for a liver problem. When he heard the problem was life threatening, Elvis received leave to fly back to Memphis where he immediately visited Gladys in the hospital. The next morning he spent several hours with her, returning that afternoon and sitting with her until almost midnight. It seemed she was not as gravely ill as he had feared (some say she perked up just at seeing her precious boy), so Elvis finally went home to get some sleep.

The phone rang at 3:30 a.m. Later, Elvis would say, "I knew what it was before I answered the telephone."

Gladys was experiencing difficulty breathing, awakening Vernon who was sleeping on a cot beside her bed. By the time a doctor could be summoned, Gladys was gone. Elvis arrived in minutes, but it was too late, and he and his father held each other, wailing their grief. Elvis couldn't be consoled; he had to be pulled from his mother's room, where he kept touching her over and over. In his despair, he called Anita, who promised to fly home from New York where she was scheduled to be on the *Andy Williams Show*.

A picture of Elvis and his father later that morning, sitting on the steps of Graceland, shows the two men with their arms around each other, looking lost and forlorn. As Elvis told a Memphis *Press-Scimitar* reporter with broken sobs, "She's all we lived for. She was always my best girl.... Now it's over." Even seeing Gladys' beloved chickens brought tears, knowing she would never feed them again. Desolate, Elvis sought out Dixie, who was now married.

Dixie recalls talking with Elvis about his mother after the funeral, rehashing what had happened when she met Gladys and how close they had become. Elvis seemed comforted by Dixie's presence, telling her how good it was to be with someone who knew him back then, when he was accepted for what he was. Despondent, he wondered aloud, "'I wonder how many of my friends who are here now would be here if it were five years ago?'" Then, Dixie says, he answered his own question. "'Not very many, because they are all looking for something from me.'"

Then, showing a spiritual side he rarely shared, Elvis told Dixie about one of his back-up singers who had "really given his heart to the Lord" after messing up his life. He had told Elvis he was going to walk away from the life he had been leading. "'I wish I could do that,'" Elvis lamented, deep sadness coloring his voice.

Dixie tried to tell Elvis he could do that, too, if he really wanted to. After all, she said, "You've already done what you wanted to do. You've been there, so just stop at the top and go back."

His voice soft and low, Elvis tried to explain it was too late. "'There are too many people [who] depend on me. I'm too obligated. I'm in too far to get out.'" As she watched him the next night, in the house full of people who came to express condolences, Dixie realized Elvis was right. "He was in it, and there was no way out."

At the service for Gladys, Elvis seemed to want it to go forever, several times sending notes back to the Blackwood Brothers, who had been Gladys' favorite quartet, asking them to sing another song. Although they had planned to sing only three or four, they had sung twelve before the notes stopped. When "Precious Memories" flooded the room, Vernon was heard to say, "All we have now are memories," and Elvis' quivering voice cried, "Oh Dad, Dad, no, no, no..." J.D. Sumner, Blackwood Brothers' bass singer, later remarked, "I have never seen a man suffer as much or grieve as much as he did at the loss of his mother."

When the service ended and Elvis went to his mother's casket for the last time, he kissed her and whispered through his tears, "Mama, I'd give up every dime I own and go back to digging ditches, just to have you back." At the gravesite, he tried to comfort his bereft father, who cried over and over that Gladys was gone and was never coming back. But at the end, Elvis collapsed over the casket, told his darling goodbye and then, as four friends helped him to the limousine, he uttered, "Oh God, everything I have is gone." Many years later, Elvis conceded he never got over Gladys' death. "The bottom dropped out of my life the day my mother died. I thought I had nothing left. In a way I was right."

Having to return to Fort Hood probably saved Elvis, although pictures show him looking dejected and lost. Germany would be a welcome escape, a new world and a new life. Elvis could no longer say to his mother, "As long as I have you." She was gone and he had the Army to serve.

# 14
# THAT'S SOMEONE YOU'LL NEVER FORGET

*Her memory is with you yet...*

~Red West

Like Vasco Smith (Maxine's husband who marched side-by-side with her in the civil rights movement), Elvis Presley found the military a great equalizer, although in a different way. As a child, the harsh reality of segregation inflicted deep wounds in Vasco's heart and mind. Yet, despite poverty, he had a dream, and for him, education was the key, just as music held the magic for Elvis' career. While Elvis' parents took him to Ellis Auditorium in Memphis to hear gospel singings, Vasco's parents took him to lectures at nearby Le Moyne College.

Even when he completed a dental degree, Vasco continued to feel the injustices all Southern blacks felt. In the army, though, his degree brought him stature and respect. There, he was equal with whites. So that's what he expected when he completed his army responsibilities and returned to Memphis about the time Elvis headed to Germany. Brown v. Board of Education had set new rules in place, but Vasco and his wife Maxine soon found rules didn't change reality.

In 1958, as Vasco struggled to escape the confines of racism as he had in the military, Elvis returned to complete his training, with the weight of his mother's untimely death heavy upon his shoulders. More than ever, he hoped the army would be a refuge from his frenetic life. He had grown tired of the constant criticism from moralistic objectors to his music and the hounding pressure of fans. With some privacy, maybe he could make friends among his fellow soldiers and perhaps do some sightseeing. For the first time in almost four years, maybe he could be *normal*.

It was not to be. Fifteen hundred fans met him at the dock in Bremerhaven, and five television crews documented his first step on

German soil, along with numerous reporters from newspapers across Europe. The frenzy he had hoped to leave behind in America had been transplanted across the Atlantic.

When he arrived in Germany, no one could believe he was genuinely going to be just "one of the guys." In fact, no one could fathom he hadn't pulled an "Eddie Fisher," using his influence as a star to get out of the army. But Elvis was committed to doing his duty like other soldiers. Initially, his job was to serve as driver for the commander of his company. That didn't last long. Three weeks later, his captain decided he couldn't handle the chaos following Elvis: reporters calling night and day and appearing unannounced; girls scaling the fence or digging under it to get to Elvis. From a customary three bags of mail a day, twenty-five bags began piling up, twenty-two of them filled with mail for Elvis.

Enough was enough; actually, it was too much. Elvis was transferred from Company D to Company C, a scout platoon, where he was out front, ready to do battle with the enemy instead of running from girls. Elvis liked being at the forefront of a different kind of action and enthusiastically embraced his new responsibilities.

To hold down disruption in the company during off-hours, Elvis was allowed to live off post, again under the guise of the dependents' policy. Predictably, that meant his family and entourage of friends and cousins could come to Germany to keep him company. This took the chaos off post, and for a few months, Elvis and his crew lived at a hotel until other guests complained about the noise and the horde of girls screaming outside. After that, they moved to a five-bedroom house, and Elvis established a regular time each day, 7:30-8:00 p.m., for autographs to give his fans access without totally disrupting his time at home. Wherever he was though, his paternal grandmother (whom Elvis called "Dodger") cooked his favorite breakfast: nine slices of burned bacon, two pints of milk, a huge bowl of gravy, and six slices of bread saturated with butter.

While the adulation of fans and the presence of his family followed him to Europe, creating a familiar environment, several major experiences occurred in Elvis' life during his two-year tour of duty in Germany that had a long-term effect on his life. The simplest change occurred in his clothing. He observed a different, sophisticated style and liked it. Soon, when he was off-duty, he had ditched his sparkly, colorful clothes from Lansky's and adopted dark suits, cut narrowly, and a white shirt and tie as his stylistic trademark. A girl on each arm of his duds didn't change—it was as if they were part of the fabric of whatever he wore.

Staying up all night partying was a habit that had followed Elvis from America. In hindsight, some of his friends say it was as if he were watching his life slip away; and consequently, he wanted to stay awake to enjoy every minute he had left. In the States, he had been able to sleep until early afternoon to make up for his late hours. In Europe, the army required him to report at daybreak. This gave rise to the second major change in life: Seeing how tired Elvis was each morning, his sergeant gave him a little pill to boost his energy level so he could stay awake on maneuvers. It didn't take long to discover two of the amphetamines could keep him going all night, and a third could get him moving when the dawn called him to duty—the pills were so magical he got some for the buddies who had come over from America to keep him company. After all, he kept them up most of the night and then demanded they get up early for breakfast with him. Harmless, Elvis said. Besides, the pills suppressed appetite so they helped maintain optimal weight—a nice side benefit to the energy acceleration that enabled Elvis and his friends to party all weekend (and most weeknights) and leave him alert and fit for duty the next morning. With money, the pills could be obtained in large quantities—quart bottles full. The supply was never ending. Elvis loved the feeling that came with the drugs—"It's all right, mama;" with a few pills, he could conquer the world. It didn't take long for his friends to notice the amphetamines also increased irritability; Elvis demanded more and more attention and was quick to show anger when he was displeased. The mood swings brought on by the pills left Elvis unpredictable, and his friends had to stay on the alert to avoid getting caught in the vortex. Red, his old high school buddy who had followed him to Europe on a whim, finally couldn't take any more and left Germany.

No one told Elvis the pills were addictive—or that they could cause heart irregularities.

The third major change in Elvis' life came when he met, through an airman named Currie Grant, the 14-year-old daughter of Captain Paul Beaulieu. Priscilla Beaulieu thought heaven had fallen in her arms when she was introduced to Elvis. She had thought about meeting him since the day her father told her he was going to be stationed in Germany. What Priscilla didn't know at the time was Elvis fell for her at least partly because he thought she resembled Debra Paget, his co-star in *Love Me Tender*. Paget had shunned him, and it still rankled. Elvis simply passed the torch he carried for Debra to Priscilla, who had similar facial features, including a button nose, as well as dark hair, styled almost the same.

At their first meeting, Elvis played the piano and sang for Priscilla. She thought he was even better looking than he was on the movie screen, but while she felt some electricity and a definite pull, it was "not in the sense that this is *it*," she recalls.

The second time they met, Elvis asked Priscilla to go to his room. Frightened, she demurred, but Elvis promised he would treat her like a sister—and he did. Elvis followed a pattern he used with all young women he truly cared about, including Dixie. Kissing and cuddling didn't breach morality, so they were acceptable. "Baby, Let's Play House" didn't apply to Priscilla, Dixie, and a few others. He controlled himself because he respected his special girls. With these chosen ones, he opened his heart, sharing his innermost thoughts and feelings. As they talked in Germany, Priscilla felt drawn to Elvis' vulnerability, his fear and uncertainty about where his life would go after the army. In turn, Elvis felt pulled toward Priscilla, sensing her empathy as well as her innocence. Soon, they were seeing each other every night. And throughout the time they spent together in Germany, Elvis remained true to his promise, even though Priscilla spent most nights in Elvis' arms in his bedroom. For Elvis, "the way she held [his] hand, the little things she planned," were enough. She was not only one of the special ones; she could be *the* one.

Early on, Priscilla perceived Elvis was two people: a little boy whose insecurity made him both vulnerable and caring and a man who could be both brutal and kind around his friends. "I really felt I got to know who Elvis Presley was during that time. Not with ego—not the star that he felt he should portray. I saw him raw, totally raw, I saw him as he really was after he lost his mother. We talked so much, he shared his grief with me...."

It was though their ages were reversed (Elvis was 24 when he met the 14-year-old charmer). Elvis acted like a child and Priscilla assumed the role of an adult. While Elvis' natural instincts emerged from music, Priscilla's instinctive strength came from human relationships and interactions. Intuitively, she knew that she and Elvis were fated to be together. Later, she would reflect on their meeting in Germany, saying, "I have gone through that night many, many times. It was a setup that was meant to be. It was something that—again, that power, that drawing power—I felt that night—I mean—what are the odds that I would ever meet Elvis Presley—in *Germany*, of all places?"

The basis of the almost instant connection, Priscilla believed, was that Elvis sensed he could be secure with her, that he could trust her. "He could talk to me about what he was feeling. And he knew I wasn't going to tell anyone. For some reason, I felt very protective of him." From fears about his future career to the loss of his mother to the obligation he felt to his fans, Elvis poured his heart out to Priscilla.

Priscilla also said Elvis felt betrayed by his father's new girlfriend Dee—someone Elvis had voiced strong objections to, defending his mother's memory by refusing to accept another woman in his father's life.

Priscilla calmed the waters for Elvis, not only providing a ready ear but also allowing Elvis to mold her into the woman of his dreams even though, or perhaps because, she was still a child. Priscilla was different from all of Elvis' other girls (whom he continued to see while dating Priscilla), and everyone, including Elvis, knew it. "Others would pass [his] way," but none would be like Priscilla because she watched and listened, and she became whatever Elvis wanted her to be.

While Priscilla and the pills were working their magic in Germany, the Colonel continued his sleights of hand back in America to keep Elvis' name and voice in the American consciousness. Elvis had recorded just enough songs to keep records coming out, but with fewer songs being released than previously, sales were declining. RCA wanted to have Elvis record in Germany, but the Colonel resisted. He was pursuing a different marketing strategy than the record label, not wanting to flood the market. At the same time, he was lining up movies for Elvis to make when he returned. By hook or crook, the Colonel kept Elvis alive and entertaining his fans while assuring that Elvis would be poised to make big bucks when he returned. He might be taking a larger share than most managers took, but he was worth it—both he and Elvis knew that, so no one complained.

For his part, Elvis prepared to change direction with his music. He spent time at the piano every night, learning new breathing techniques and ways to expand his vocal range. Drawn by his heart to the ballads he had loved but had mostly abandoned, he dreamed of being able to take a song where Roy Hamilton had taken "You'll Never Walk Alone." He studied Hamilton and other ballad singers, never forgetting the Caruso records he had been fascinated with as a child. For Elvis, singing ballads was a passion; he lived the stories as he sang them. The Colonel was pumped and on board (he had never really liked rock 'n' roll)—working with RCA, he engineered carefully crafted news releases hinting at Elvis' new style.

Even as excited as he was about a new vocal direction, Elvis' most important goal was to become a serious actor. He and the Colonel agreed movies were the best long-term security, but they didn't agree on the kind of movies it would take to achieve that aspiration. Elvis wanted dramatic roles with no singing; the Colonel wanted light-hearted movies with songs to whet the appetite of record buyers.

Although they differed on the vehicle, Elvis and the Colonel agreed an image change was essential. The criticism that had hit a high note before Elvis joined the Army could not be reignited upon his return to America. Allegations that he contributed to juvenile delinquency had to be avoided this time around. They had had a good ride, and Elvis knew he had been lucky. "I happened to come along at a time in the music business when there was no trend. The people were looking for something different, and I was lucky. I came along just in time." The generational timing accounted for a large portion of the criticism, but it still hurt. Moving away from the concert stage seemed a good solution. Elvis added that he would miss his singing career, but he was keyed up about going a different way in a different venue.

## THAT'S SOMEONE YOU'LL NEVER FORGET

His hitch was just about up, and Elvis had served his time honorably, even earning his sergeant's stripes; he was ready to go home and pick up his career. He had only one problem: Priscilla—the love of his life. As Keogh wrote, Elvis and Priscilla were opposite-sex versions of each other. Priscilla's dark hair and sparkling eyes resembled these same physical traits in Elvis. Keogh adds that the physical likeness may have been the silent, underlying attraction, but Elvis' connection with Priscilla approached the level of karmic. Whether fate or the hand of God, Priscilla came into Elvis' life when he needed someone to replace his precious mother—someone who cared about him with every fiber of her being. For Priscilla, a young woman inexperienced in the ways of the world and of love, Elvis sparkled like a star. She saw a man who adored her and wanted to protect her. Her view was idealized—she saw a handsome idol who let her enter his blessed life.

How could she live without him? And how could he face an uncertain future without her at his side? He promised he would send for her, and she wanted to believe he would—he was "someone you never forget." Elvis *knew* she would wait for him.

Even after marriage and divorce, the lyrics would still ring true: "Others may pass your way and let you think their love is true, but you know that they'll never replace the one that waits for you." For the moment, though, all she had was his army jacket, which he had left with her.

The picture of Priscilla at the airport where she had rushed to see Elvis off shows a heartbroken young girl, a scarf covering her dark hair on the cold, overcast day. The caption read, "The Girl He Left Behind." How wrong that was.

# 15
# FLAMING STAR

*And so I ride, front of that flaming star*

*Never lookin' around...*

~Sid Wayne

What a homecoming! Met by the Colonel, Nancy Sinatra (representing her father, who couldn't be present), and RCA executives (as well as a horde of reporters, of course), Elvis talked willingly about serving his country. But that was behind him; he was home and ready to get back in gear. No one said it, but the Colonel and Elvis hoped the Army break had erased his vicious, negative public perception. It was going to be a new day in glory; and fresh off a tour of duty for his country, it was going to be unsullied and positive.

A whistle-stop train trip to Memphis with screaming girls at every station provided evidence Elvis had not been forgotten. The returning star presented his new image in a press conference before fifty-plus reporters at Graceland. Dressed in a Continental-style suit, still black but without his trademark colors adding dash, Elvis looked the part of a young, cosmopolitan male. Gone was the black pomaded hair; in its place his natural light brown color with a more casual yet dramatic upsweep. In keeping with the cleaned-up image, behind Elvis a plaque displayed his religious underpinnings: "Let not your heart be troubled. Ye who believe in God believe also in Me."

Not surprisingly, on Elvis' first full day at home he visited his mother's grave, where the inscription on her tombstone conveyed his innermost love: "She was the Sunshine of our Home." Still despondent over his mother's death, his father's impending marriage, which he thought flagrantly disrespected Gladys' memory, added to Elvis' desolation.

Getting back to work helped, but Elvis returned again and again to his mother's gravesite, a gesture of love and sadness in the midst of a life where he felt the insecurity of knowing most people who loved him really only loved his generosity. Perhaps that's why he brought his young secretary, Elizabeth, back to America with him. She treated him like a real person. Elizabeth adored Elvis, serving as more than a secretary, even hiding a half-gallon jug of amphetamines in her luggage on the flight to America so he would have a quick supply until he could find new sources.

Life in America returned to a regular routine, with cousins Gene and Billy ever present, along with Junior Smith and George Klein. Fans reappeared at the gates of Graceland as if they had never been gone. Elvis returned to his gift-giving mode, buying cars for his friends, including a new yellow Lincoln for Elizabeth, although unknown to him, her attraction was moving to Elvis' friend Rex as she realized she was one among many with Elvis.

On the business front, RCA wanted to produce an album, *Elvis Is Back*, to coincide with an upcoming *Sinatra* show. In Nashville, the usual tape and play, tape and play went forward, resulting in several songs that would become hits, including "Stuck on You," "Fame and Fortune," and "Soldier Boy." The one song of the session that showed Elvis' ability to escape staleness and add his own style was "A Mess of Blues." Guralnick says it reflected Elvis unpredictability and his playful sense of fun, suggesting a return to the unfettered freedom that had added zest to Elvis' music from the beginning. "It was tailored to his image without being confined to it, and Elvis' high-spirited whoop at the end, a kind of wobbly falsetto, is almost reminiscent of his joyous exclamation at the conclusion of 'Mystery Train,'" he notes.

After the recording sessions, Elvis dyed his hair black so it would be more striking for the taping of the *Sinatra* show, which was going to take place in Florida. Scotty recalled the trip drew so many fans along the way—streets lined with people in little towns everywhere—that it was as triumphal as the trip home from the Army, or even the return of the star to his hometown of Tupelo, Mississippi, several years earlier.

Scotty and D.J. were thankful to be back in the fold, but they were taken aback when Elvis offered them a couple of little white pills, which Scotty says he never took. Joe Esposito, whom Elvis had met in Germany, had joined the entourage, assuming the same role of helping

Elvis he had played overseas. Some of the guys felt displaced by Joe, who had stolen their standing of closeness with Elvis. When he invited Joe to share a two-bedroom suite with him, it stung. Now, not only was the Colonel keeping the old gang at arm's length, but Elvis was also committing acts of betrayal.

The new Elvis hadn't abandoned all of his suggestive stage movements, but on the *Sinatra* show, the hip gyrations had been replaced with a smoother, fluid body rhythm in time with the music. In a conservative tuxedo, he sang Sinatra's own "Witchcraft," partly as a duet with the older man, and "Fame and Fortune," a ballad. Sinatra crooned through "Love Me Tender," and again the two ended the song as a duet in pleasing, soulful harmony. On faster songs like "Stuck on You," Elvis snapped his fingers, but his leg didn't jiggle.

Elvis was a little older than when he left for Germany, and his fan base had matured as he had. The new Elvis was a perfect fit. The show garnered a 67.7 percent audience share. Elvis was back, and his fans' devotion had survived his two-year absence.

Like Sinatra, he had changed with the times. Unlike Sinatra, he had retained his sexiness, and Sinatra didn't miss the possibility that associating with Elvis would pump his own ratings, which had been in a slump.

Back in the recording studio in Nashville, for the first time "Boots" Randolph joined the lineup of back-up musicians. In keeping with Elvis' appreciation for a wide genre of songs, he recorded blues and ballads, as well as pop tunes. But it was "Are You Lonesome Tonight?" that seized his emotions, prompting him to start speaking lines rather than singing them. Recorded at the request of the Colonel (which was unusual), the song captured the hearts of fans overnight, rising to #2 on *Billboards'* Hot 100 Chart in the second week before rising to #1, where it stayed for six weeks. It was also #1 in England for four weeks. Showing Elvis could still reach diverse audiences, the song hit #22 on the country chart and #3 on the R&B chart.

That same night, while playing around, Elvis recorded "Reconsider Baby," which Guralnick pinpoints as indicative of how Elvis' soaring voice gives the blues a kind of abandon in which harmony runs the gamut in the genre, adding that it pulls up thoughts of Little Junior

Parker. In the end, though, Guralnick says the sound is pure Elvis. What makes his mark even more amazing is that he did it "his way" in whatever genre he was singing. Elvis was a man who lived almost every song he sang—he sang from his soul. Listeners felt the connection he had with a song, and they in turn connected with him.

In the same way Elvis touched his audience when he sang, he wanted to relate to them from the movie screen. He didn't object when scripts were reworked to add similarities to his own life. *Jailhouse Rock* was no exception. The third and final film under contract with Hal Wallis, this movie wove Elvis' life into the singer Tulsa McLean, who finishes his tour of duty in the army in the movie. The location was moved to Germany for an additional connection and included some of the touristy scenes shot when Hal Wallis visited Elvis there. The movie was a perfect vehicle for calling attention to Elvis' service to his country, and naturally, the Colonel capitalized on the positive publicity that had been generated during the time Elvis was stationed in overseas.

The next film, *G. I. Blues*, differs in several ways from Elvis' previous movies. First, it took the form of a musical comedy rather than a musical drama. Gone this time is the show business success story, replaced by a love theme in which Elvis and his leading lady have conflicting opinions about the singer's settling down to family life. Also not present is the hip-swinging, leg-jiggling singing performance. Elvis is transformed, just as he was in real life, into a clean-cut young soldier with short hair, minus his sideburns and provocative attitude. As an actor, he didn't mind the changes to his appearance or even those to his stage performance, but he felt the absence of his rebel image in the movie went too far. The rebel in him defined "his way." Without it, the iconographic, branded trademark was incomplete. The Colonel thought the move essential, but Elvis thought he was losing the "real" person he had been all his life.

Combined with the dissension over the music, the loss of the rebel image underscored that Elvis and the Colonel saw a different path to his continued stardom, and it was becoming a sore point between the two. Even so, Elvis reminded himself, the Colonel helped him get to the pinnacle of the music world, and he had managed to keep his fans intact during his two-year hiatus. In short, he owed him, so he went along.

# MY WAY

Without the Colonel, he might have to go back to driving a truck. When he thought about standing up to the Colonel, he felt "that flaming star over his shoulder," so he rode with the Colonel, "front of that flaming star," trying to "never look around."

Elvis gave in on a lot, but he refused to leave his hair its natural color, perhaps because his hero James Dean had coal black hair, although some think it was because he mother had dyed her hair black. For the first time, the movie was shot in color, and Elvis' dyed black hair is striking, clearly a change from his natural color. The previous films, in black and white, failed to show the dramatic difference.

Lastly, the music in the film, while fast, is subdued compared to some of Elvis' most strident songs. No longer hard driving, Elvis' sound has lost its hiccupping effect and much of its regional baggage.

Even to fans looking for the old Elvis, *G. I. Blues* answered their call for more of Elvis' magic. The movie ranked 14th in box-office receipts in 1960, and the album featuring the title song and "Wooden Heart," a ballad, had staying power on the charts—longer than any other Elvis album. The financial success failed to placate Elvis. Even positive reviews by the media couldn't lift him from the doldrums. This film flopped at meeting his personal criteria—serious acting. And the music still appeared superfluous, with most of the songs adding nothing to the plot line.

On the other hand, Elvis loved Hollywood, where partying all night was the norm. He began to act like the Godfather, demanding loyalty or pay the price. His entourage had to look and act the part of supporting cast. Soon the hangers-on, known as the Memphis Mafia, found themselves clothed in dark duds and deeply colored sunglasses. The TCB insignia was used on everything from the sunglasses to pendants, which all of the Memphis Mafia had received as gifts. Elvis even provided briefcases so the gang would look professional—or at least look like they had something to do besides hang out with him. Of course, what was in the briefcases hinted at the truth. Gene's reportedly had a hairbrush and a doorknob, and he made no bones about admitting he really didn't do anything. He boldly asserted his claim to fame was being one of Elvis' cousins.

All in all, it was a fun life. Hanging out with Bobby Darin, Sammy

MY WAY

Without the Colonel, he might have to go back to driving a truck. When he thought about standing up to the Colonel, he felt "that flaming star over his shoulder," so he rode with the Colonel, "front of that flaming star," trying to "never look around."

Elvis gave in on a lot, but he refused to leave his hair its natural color, perhaps because his hero James Dean had coal black hair, although some think it was because he mother had dyed her hair black. For the first time, the movie was shot in color, and Elvis' dyed black hair is striking, clearly a change from his natural color. The previous films, in black and white, failed to show the dramatic difference.

Lastly, the music in the film, while fast, is subdued compared to some of Elvis' most strident songs. No longer hard driving, Elvis' sound has lost its hiccupping effect and much of its regional baggage.

Even to fans looking for the old Elvis, *G. I. Blues* answered their call for more of Elvis' magic. The movie ranked 14th in box-office receipts in 1960, and the album featuring the title song and "Wooden Heart," a ballad, had staying power on the charts—longer than any other Elvis album. The financial success failed to placate Elvis. Even positive reviews by the media couldn't lift him from the doldrums. This film flopped at meeting his personal criteria—serious acting. And the music still appeared superfluous, with most of the songs adding nothing to the plot line.

On the other hand, Elvis loved Hollywood, where partying all night was the norm. He began to act like the Godfather, demanding loyalty or pay the price. His entourage had to look and act the part of supporting cast. Soon the hangers-on, known as the Memphis Mafia, found themselves clothed in dark duds and deeply colored sunglasses. The TCB insignia was used on everything from the sunglasses to pendants, which all of the Memphis Mafia had received as gifts. Elvis even provided briefcases so the gang would look professional—or at least look like they had something to do besides hang out with him. Of course, what was in the briefcases hinted at the truth. Gene's reportedly had a hairbrush and a doorknob, and he made no bones about admitting he really didn't do anything. He boldly asserted his claim to fame was being one of Elvis' cousins.

All in all, it was a fun life. Hanging out with Bobby Darin, Sammy

108

# FLAMING STAR

Davis, Jr., Nick Adams, and a string of Hollywood starlets, they laughed and talked most of the night and then had to be up by 5 a.m. to be on the set with Elvis—which he absolutely insisted on. By now, all of the guys lived on amphetamines; they had to if they had any hope of keeping up with Elvis.

Doll questions why Elvis felt the need to surround himself with an army of "buddy-bodyguards" and surmises a comment Elvis made to *Tropic* magazine may hold the key: "The trouble is, when a fellow is by himself and starts thinking, the bad things are always stronger in his memory than the happy things."

About this time, Elvis developed an interest in karate and began taking lessons from Ed Parker, a well-known master of the art in Hollywood. Parker recalls Elvis' sharing how his mother had kept him in a protective cocoon in his youth, away from sports as much as she could. Now that she wasn't around to worry about him, he was excited about finding release in an activity that would challenge him mentally and physically.

Vernon's marriage to Dee in July of that year (1960) left Elvis needing karate—or at least something—to deal with his sense of despondence. Back in Memphis after the shooting of *G. I. Blues* ended, he tried to pretend everything was normal, even after his father brought his bride, along with her three children, home to Graceland. Publicly, Elvis played the role of a good son who wanted his father to be happy, but he made it clear he would never look at Dee as his mother. Gladys was the only mother he would ever have—and that was that. Alone, with Dee in his parents' bedroom, he felt an impenetrable fog hanging over the whole house. Soon, he decided he would spend the time off before his next film in Vegas, and he hit the road. Before he left, in an interview with the Memphis *Press-Scimitar*, Elvis revealed his true feelings: "He is my father, and he's all I've got left in the world. He stood by me all these years and sacrificed things he wanted so that I could have clothes and lunch money to go to school. I'll stand by him now—right or wrong."

The only bright spot in Elvis' life was his upcoming film, *Flaming Star* (originally titled *Black Star*). After four films, at last he had the opportunity for some serious acting—this would be dramatic, no silly songs interrupting the dialogue, he was told, although the final

109

production had two. Thrilled he had been selected for a starring role originally conceived for Marlon Brando, Elvis threw himself into the role of Pacer, a man caught between two races, a half-breed comfortable in neither world. Sadly, the director showed little respect for Elvis (he had been opposed to Elvis in the role), and this reopened Elvis' insecurity, making it impossible for him to get a grasp on the level of acting required. Some say the "uppers" Elvis was taking had as much to do with his lackluster performance as the patronizing director did. Even the producer, David Weisbart, said Elvis had lost his greatest asset, "his natural ability," and consequently "flounders about instead for some stock theatrical gesture." Weisbart had believed in Elvis (he was the one who pushed the director to use him), but he conceded the film "never really [gives] Elvis a chance to rise above a style of ensemble acting for which he is clearly not suited." He added that Elvis never got "beyond a somewhat passive, reactive response."

Doll asserts that *Flaming Star*, despite Elvis' missteps, remained a "well-crafted, highly watchable western," due mainly to the good work of other cast members and the crew. The script itself came from a popular novel by Clair Huffaker, and the screenwriter known for his scripting of *The Grapes of Wrath* (Nunnelly Johnson), co-wrote the film version with Huffaker.

Although not molded from Elvis' life like some of his earlier movies, *Flaming Star* ends with a scene that might have been a premonition. At the end, the central character Pacer, wounded beyond healing, saw the "flaming star of death" and rode into the desert to die. Before he took his last breath, he whispered, "Maybe someday, somewhere, people'll understand folks like us."

Elvis stayed ahead of the flaming star a while longer. Seeing it over his shoulder, he sings, "There's a lot of livin' I've got to do. Give me time to make a few dreams come true, flaming star." The flaming star wouldn't come down on him yet.

# 16
# SOUND ADVICE

*Some folks tell you what to do*
*They insist they know more than you*

~Bernie Baum and Bill Giant

Springtime, 1960, after he wrapped up *Flaming Star*, Elvis spent a lively weekend in Vegas before returning to the home he no longer felt was home. Even at home, he was homesick. Perhaps seeking solace, he decided to record a gospel album in Nashville. But his excitement about the new album couldn't keep his nightmares away. In a recurring one, Colonel Parker was missing and Elvis felt fearful, alone and deserted. The recording session itself, though, awakened his spiritual leanings, and he poured his heart into "His Hand in Mine," "I Believe in the Man in the Sky," and "He Knows Just What I Need." His spirit rejuvenated, Elvis headed to Los Angeles to record the soundtrack for his next picture, *Wild in the Country*.

This time the Colonel insisted on more songs, even though the story line was melodramatic. The strongest attribute of Elvis' performance was not the four songs he sang—it was his soul mate connection with Tuesday Weld, who played one of the women in Glenn Tyler's [Elvis'] life. The connection between the two was instant and unmistakable, and their screen performances caught the chemistry.

Few critics think Elvis gave his best performance in *Wild in the Country*, but the film's seriousness at addressing the important themes of poverty, class, and crime make it a reputable strength in his film career. Regrettably, some discount that, implying Elvis never caught the substance of his character, while others inferred he didn't even try, seeming indifferent to the role he was playing. His perfunctory performance lacked depth, and for once, his charisma did not carry him.

The strongest criticism came from Elvis himself. He knew he had failed in his foray into dramatic roles, and he didn't understand why.

Those closest to him wondered if his performance, like his behavior, was erratic because of the influence of amphetamines. Increasingly, Elvis vacillated from generous and giving to foul or furious tempers where he attacked everyone in sight for their lack of loyalty. The mood swings were worrisome, but no one knew what to do. If only his mother were alive, she could talk to Elvis, get him back on the right track. Without her guiding force, Elvis resisted advice, even it if was sound.

Because *Flaming Star* and *Wild in the Country* failed to hit the box office at the level of Elvis' first three movies, the Colonel overruled Elvis and insisted he return to musical comedies loaded with songs. In the interim, the Colonel came up with the idea for a charity concert to help construct a memorial to honor the 1,102 officers and enlisted men who had gone down with their ship, the *U.S.S. Arizona*, when the Japanese bombed Pearl Harbor. An earlier benefit in Memphis had brought significant positive media, and the Colonel wanted a repeat performance. Elvis would play a concert in Hawaii, with all proceeds going to the memorial fund. Not even expenses would be deducted.

The Colonel wanted the benefit concert in Hawaii to be bigger and better than the one in Memphis, which the Memphis *Commercial Appeal* had touted as a melting pot of music, from "Negro cotton field harmony, camp meeting fervor, Hollywood showmanship, beatnik nonchalance, and some of the manipulations of mass psychology." The other Memphis paper, the *Press-Scimitar*, reported a "new edge of irony" in Elvis' performance, and one of the Jordanaires, Ray Walker, discerned a "kind of effervescence about him."

The Memphis concert was pure benefit; the one in Hawaii had a dual purpose: raise money for the memorial and build excitement about the filming of *Blue Hawaii*, the first of the lighter movies being demanded by the colonel. Before heading to the Hawaii benefit, Elvis had a recording session in Nashville where his new vision for ballads made its debut, striking gold. Two songs, according to Guralnick, offered Elvis an unusual occasion for contemplation and interpretation in a more serious mode. "There's Always Me" and "Starting Today" struck a new chord. The songwriter for "There's Always Me," Don Robertson, sat in on the recording session and remembers how Elvis sang the ending: "He got almost operatic." It reminded Robertson of how Elvis soared on "It's

Now or Never." Minnie Pearl, who accompanied Elvis on the plane to Hawaii, was afraid it was "now," not "never," as they stepped off the plane. "There is no way to describe the pandemonium. I never saw as many women in my life. They were screaming. They were yelling. I was just horrified. I thought, 'They're going to kill him.' And they would have if they could have gotten loose, I'm afraid."

Unfazed, Elvis told her, "They're not going to hurt me." He fed on his fans' frenzy, and by the time he hit the stage that night, the deep, throaty thrill of joy in joining his audience in an emotional high could not be contained. Another of the Jordanaires, Gordon Stoker, said the "spontaneity to his performance closely resembled a man being let out of jail."

Despite the glimpse of the "old" Elvis, it would be his last public concert for eight long years.

And while Elvis went from financial success to financial success, the passion seemed missing on the big screen. The Colonel's greed drove the creation of multi-media vehicles for his star, but they lit no flame for Elvis. Clearly, the spark seen in *King Creole* and *Love Me Tender* faded in *Blue Hawaii* and other movies. It's not that the 14 songs in *Blue Hawaii* and the tunes in other movies are not masterfully delivered; it is that Elvis clearly doesn't feel comfortable in roles where songs are superimposed over the story line. He simply isn't able to control or camouflage his insecurity and turmoil. At times, he garbles lines and at others, the level of his intensity is misplaced. Elvis biographer Guralnick says Elvis almost seems embarrassed and exasperated he can't make what was once so natural in his movements fit the silly songs he is forced to sing. His music trivialized, Elvis tries, but he is unable to hide his shame.

Sadly, the financial success of *Blue Hawaii* relegated Elvis to musical comedies, which he detested. He had capitulated, no longer going "his way." The Colonel had worked out a formula that guaranteed money: Record a soundtrack from the movie to be released as a record by RCA. It was a win-win—the movie helped record sales, and the record increased attendance at the movie.

The irony of the Colonel's successful channeling of America's musical rebel was reflected in the lyrics of the tamed down songs. "Some folks like to be the boss; they get up on their high horse." But Elvis knew, "They insist that they're givin' sound advice, but as sure as you're livin', it ain't sound, it ain't nice." If he had been more self-assured, he would have thought twice, but without anyone on his side, he didn't have the strength. He was in a rut and couldn't get out. Still, several of the movies gave Elvis some of his most popular songs, including "Can't Help Falling in Love" from *Blue Hawaii*.

Although Elvis had high hopes for the cinematic partnership with producer Hal Wallis, whose films received 16 Academy Award nominations, Wallis saw Elvis as a consistent moneymaker rather than as a serious actor. Following *Blue Hawaii*, Elvis would star in another 23 films, eight produced by Wallis, all financially successful, but disappointing to the striving kid from Tupelo who dreamed of being a dramatic actor. Elvis later reflected on the partnership with Wallis, calling him a "double-dealing sonofabitch," bitter about the crushing of his dream.

Elvis' musical movies, invariably comedies, were predictable: The star, even if he moved like marionette on a string, had an exciting job (e.g., racing cars in *Viva Las Vegas, Spinout,* and *Speedway*; performing in a rodeo in *Stay Away, Joe* and *Tickle Me*; piloting a small aircraft in *It Happened at the World's Fair* and *Paradise, Hawaiian Style*). He worked in famous, sometimes glamorous locations like Hawaii, Las Vegas, Acapulco, and even London. And, except for two of the movies (*Kissin' Cousins* and *Blue Hawaii*), after his return from the army the characters Elvis played no longer had their roots in the South, another move away from Elvis' real life. To make Elvis more broadly appealing, the goal, according to Doll, was to wipe out—albeit without fanfare, his Southern identity.

Another common feature of the musical comedies centered on the romantic ventures of the star, which often went from the screen to real life in Elvis' bedroom. But along with the lovely leading ladies, often Elvis' characters touched other hearts, usually of women or children.

The best of these movies, Doll claims, are *Viva Las Vegas*, 1964, co-starring Ann-Margret (this film was Elvis' highest-grossing film); *Roustabout*, released just after *Viva*, also in 1964, with Barbara Stanwyck; *Girl Happy*, 1965, with Shelly Fabares; and *Speedway*, released in 1968, co-

SOUND ADVICE

starring Nancy Sinatra. Among the worst were *Tickle Me*, which was released just after *Girl Happy* in 1965; *Frankie and Johnny*, 1966; and *Clambake*, 1967, all of which were shot in record time, leaving little time for rehearsal and shaving weeks of shooting and thus costs. Other money-saving strategies instituted by Parker resulted in those and other movies being shortchanged: shooting on location virtually disappeared, with studio shots from old sets often used; the number of shots and retakes were reduced to a minimum; and, the quality of soundtrack albums diminished. For *Tickle Me*, the Colonel even offered old recordings to avoid the cost of cutting new soundtracks. Even so, despite the devil in the details of quality, *Tickle Me* brought in the third highest revenues in the history of Allied Artists, the small production company that released it. For fans, if Elvis was on the screen, that was all that mattered; they came in droves.

The low point of Elvis' film career, Doll declares, is *Kissin' Cousins*, a "quickie" film produced by Sam Katzman. Not only were only 15 days allowed for shooting, the script patronized Southerners, capitalizing on stereotypical images of hillbillies cavorting around barefooted, moonshiners stirring their brew, and sluggish hound dogs sleeping under unpainted porches.

The Elvis publicity machine, orchestrated by Colonel Parker, used these formulaic movies to reposition Elvis from a teenage pop idol to a star more acceptable to his maturing audience. Like the teenage pop stars (Justin Timberlake, Britney Spears, or Christina Aguilera) who followed him, Elvis had to reach out to his changing audience. The ravening teenie-boppers had grown older, as had Elvis, and his appearance and behavior had to comply. The suave dresser who returned from Europe fit the bill. In an interview with the *Australasian Post*, Elvis said he couldn't believe he "had actually ever worn some of the gaudy shirts and sports jackets," adding he didn't want to look like a hick anymore. Living in Hollywood as much as he did in Memphis helped wipe out such hillbilly images. Media coverage of his generosity established him as a solid citizen who helped his fellowman. Lastly, press conferences were highly orchestrated, and impromptu interviews were no longer allowed. Whenever possible, news releases with quotes by Elvis substituted for direct contact with media.

Between films, Elvis seemed eager to get back in the recording studio, where he had more freedom from the Colonel and could do it "his way" most of the time. He continued to forge his maturing artistic identity, pouring his emotions into the latest path he had chosen. Guralnick described Elvis' new direction in the early 1960s as "composed of equal parts bravado (the aria-like quality of many of his most ambitious songs) and vulnerability (the utterly naked, painfully wounded fragility of some of the Don Robertson and Doc Pomus ballads)." The recording sessions stood in stark contrast to the artistically humiliating music he recorded for his "silly" movies. But they weren't consistently high notes. Gordon Stoker said Elvis' frustration sometimes showed in the studio, but in the end, Elvis would give up, admit defeat and just do the best he could when he was faced with sorry music. When that happened, "just as sure as you're livin'," his soul strength was weak, and he did what the "boss" advised.

The magic was gone. Doll notes that between 1960 and 1968, not one of Elvis' recordings made it on the country charts. None of his songs made it to the R&B charts again after 1963. He had one top-ten single, "Crying in the Chapel," in 1965 (it had actually been recorded in 1960) and one song that made it to the top 20 in 1966, "Love Letters."

A large part of the problem was that the Colonel's wheeling and dealing to maximize profits limited Elvis almost totally to songs from Hill and Range, RCA's publishing house, whose writers seemed out of tune with the music of the day. Plus, with the cutthroat deal Hill and Range had been forced to sign, they gave up royalties, so there was little incentive to get their creative juices flowing.

Elvis' edge as a singer was floundering, compromised by insipid material, and he knew it.

He hid his creative frustration with high profile romantic flings, pinballing from one girl to another. In their hands, he willingly let his "heart [be] clay, to take and hold as [they] may."

But Priscilla was coming to visit, and life was about to get complicated.

# 16

# ANY WAY YOU WANT ME TO BE

*Yes, any way you want me,*

*Well, that's how I will be.*

~Aaron Schroeder

Priscilla waved goodbye to Elvis when he left Germany and wondered fearfully if the whirlwind had disappeared from her life. When Elvis called three weeks later, she felt like a shooting star had fallen at her feet. He remembered her! It was weeks before she heard from him again, but as long as he kept calling, she didn't care how long she had to wait. Between calls, she wrote him long letters—usually daily—and he occasionally sent her one of his new records. Priscilla found them as convincing as love letters—"Sealed with a Kiss," "Good Night, My Love," and other romantic songs with messages especially for her.

In 1962, when Elvis invited Priscilla to fly to America to visit him, her parents took some convincing—and a number of promises—but Elvis was equal to the task. At his most charming, he assured them Priscilla would be well chaperoned. And she was, by the whole Memphis Mafia and their wives. That was not exactly what the Captain had expected. He thought Priscilla would be staying with George Barris (the man who customized Elvis' cars and other vehicles) and his wife. What he didn't know couldn't hurt him, Elvis later rationalized.

Arriving in Los Angeles, the 17-year-old Priscilla was surprised when Joe Esposito, not Elvis, picked her up at the airport and drove her to the house Elvis had rented in Hollywood. She felt better when Elvis greeted her with a kiss in front of all of his buddies as he momentarily paused from playing pool. After introductions, though, he turned back to the pool table, leaving Priscilla feeling like a fifth wheel, although he did occasionally amble over and plant another kiss on her lips.

In Hollywood, Elvis seemed like a different person, and Priscilla

117

panicked: Had she miscalculated his interest in her? Was he merely infatuated with her and wanted her around to show off? Or, was the love she had felt in Germany hidden beneath the layer of confidence Elvis had adopted in front of his friends? Was their love real, or had it been a figment of her imagination? The questions spun like a record turntable in her mind. Disconcerted, she feared coming to America had been a mistake—what if Elvis used her and tossed her aside? She had heard rumors about all of the girls he loved and then discarded...was she going to be the next in a long line?

All her doubts faded when they finally went to Elvis' room. Wrapped in his arms, she felt secure in his love. In her arms, *his* insecurity resurfaced. He became the vulnerable, needy man with whom she had fallen in love in Germany. She was ready to give him her all—but Elvis insisted he had too much respect for her to go all the way. "'Not yet, not now. We have a lot to look forward to. I'm not going to spoil you. There'll be a right time and place, and when the time comes, I'll know it.'"

"Although confused," Priscilla conceded later, "I wasn't about to argue. He made it clear that this was what he wanted. He made it sound so romantic, and, in a strange way, it *was* something to look forward to...." That night he had Joe take Priscilla to the Barris' home to ensure he kept his promise to her father.

Before she left to return home to Germany a couple of weeks later, Elvis reminded Priscilla he would know if she didn't keep herself pure for him. "'I want you back the way you are now,'" he instructed. "'And remember, I'll always know.'" Priscilla understood that she would only be acceptable to him if he had her "his way."

Chastity didn't mean the two of them weren't going to have fun during her visit to America, and Vegas was the place to show her his definition of fun. (Obviously, the commitment to Priscilla's mother and stepfather about staying with the Barris' had been shelved.) For two weeks, they played and partied far into the night, with the young Priscilla having an eye-opening experience—from a new wardrobe and hairstyle accentuated by heavy make-up to learning that pills put you to sleep and perked you up the next morning when you felt washed out. She also learned what triggered Elvis' mood swings: "There were

ANY WAY YOU WANT ME TO BE

definitely rules. You had to play by the rules. The more you knew, the longer you lasted."

The Priscilla who returned to Europe two weeks after she left wasn't much older, but she was light years wiser. So was Anita Wood, who, despite Elvis' efforts to keep her in the dark, learned about Priscilla's visit. Devastated, Anita finally accepted her first love would not be her last—that Elvis cherished her but she alone was not enough to satisfy him. Looking back, Anita said, "I was in my young twenties and I was ready to get married and have a family, and then the fact that this little girl [had come] all the way over from Germany—I mean I couldn't believe it. So I just made the decision. It was a very difficult decision because I loved him...and I hated to give up being with him, enjoying the fun and the super things that we did, because I knew there would never be anyone like that again or any way of life like that again—but I was ready for that step."

Elvis struggled with Anita's decision, but in the end, he released her, saying he prayed to God he was doing the right thing. Candidly, Elvis later admitted he was not only sad but relieved—"hiding" Priscilla filled him with guilt. As he sang so tenderly, he had "found a new love and [would] always want her near." Still, in many ways Anita was the last link with his mother, who had loved her like a daughter. But, Elvis was sure Mama would have loved Priscilla, too. She always cherished whomever Elvis loved. Besides, the next time Priscilla visited, he could bring her to Graceland without worrying about Anita.

It didn't take long—six months after she returned to Germany, Elvis invited Priscilla to his home for Christmas. Once again, it took his special persuasive powers, including a promise that she would stay with his father and stepmother. When Priscilla arrived, Vernon and Dee met her in New York and accompanied her to Memphis. But on this visit she didn't have to meet the king in a pool room—Elvis had his dad call him when they were close and he rushed to pick Priscilla up so he would be at her side the first time she rode through the gates of Graceland.

To help Priscilla sleep after her long trip, Elvis gave her a couple of pills, too much for her tiny body. Two days later, she woke up wondering why everyone had been concerned about her, not realizing she'd slept for 48 hours. Just one pill perked Priscilla up. From that

119

point, the visit was a blitz, with Elvis giving her the grand tour of Memphis, introducing her to his friends, and even renting an entire movie theatre so they could watch what they wanted without a flock of fans encircling them. New Year's Eve came and went in a blur of alcohol, and suddenly it was time for Priscilla to leave. Beside himself, Elvis begged her parents to let her stay longer, and when his winning ways failed to move Captain Beaulieu, Elvis lost it, going into a rage. In the end, Priscilla left as scheduled, but this time she didn't have to worry about Elvis forgetting her. He called virtually every night, and their conversation centered on how he could get her back in the United States. He was obsessed.

The plan was to convince her parents to let her come to Memphis to finish high school. The Captain declared war, but Elvis didn't just defend his proposition; he took an offensive stance. The Captain thought General Patton had returned—the tactical and logistical maneuvers by Elvis, combined with intercession by Priscilla's mother (who feared the fighting was tearing up the family), left the Captain with no choice except surrender. The Captain did insist on coming with Priscilla to personally supervise the arrangements for her care and protection.

Less than three months after she left Memphis, Priscilla was back, presumably to stay with the elder Presley, although that only lasted as long as her father was in town. Elvis almost had second thoughts, realizing he might be giving up the freedom to have any girl he chose, but in the end, he knew Priscilla was "the one" he could conform to "his way." With care and concern, he would train her to be the woman of his dreams. She was young enough not to resist, accepting his teaching and direction as her calling to serve him. In his hands, her heart was clay "to take and hold as you may."

Thousands of miles from her family, Priscilla had some lonely days. A new school, new friends, a new family—and it seemed Elvis was never home. He constantly took off to Hollywood or someplace else to film a movie, and that always brought rumors of girls on his arm and in his bedroom. The latest was Ursula Andress, and Priscilla tried to believe Elvis' denials. He was so sweet, always bringing her the nicest gifts when he came home—last time it was a fire-engine-red Corvair. Was he feeling guilty about being unfaithful to her, she wondered, or was he just trying to please her, making her feel special?

Amazingly, other than in Memphis, most of the media hounds didn't know Priscilla existed; and the few who did accepted his explanation that she was a young girl staying with his family until her military family returned to America.

When Elvis was home, he continued to mold Priscilla into his ideal image, including having porcelain caps put on her teeth and persuading her to dye her hair black like his by telling her it would make her blue eyes stand out more. Once on Union Avenue in Memphis, he spent four hours watching her try on outfit after outfit, offering a running commentary on what suited her and what didn't. He had specific tastes for her in style and color. No prints or patterns, he declared, because Priscilla would look lost in them. They would take attention away from *her*. And, of course, he wanted a perfect fit. When they left the shop with dozens of shopping bags, Priscilla had been transformed from a simple young girl to a sophisticated, stylish grown-up—at least in appearance.

Years later, Priscilla recalled that shopping spree—and others—with a sharper perspective. In hindsight, she realized, "I was Elvis' doll, his own living doll, to fashion as he pleased." At the time, she accepted it without question.

Sometimes, though, she felt confused and unsettled. When she was with Elvis, most of the time he treated her like a queen. She lived in a castle, and the king loved her more than any of the mistresses in other cities. But occasionally the person Priscilla used to be—the one who didn't quake the first time she met Elvis, the one who had an independent streak—sneaked out when she wasn't expecting it. On one of those occasions, she walked into a salon and had her hair cut.

"'How could you cut your goddamn hair? You know I like long hair.'" Crestfallen, Priscilla realized she had broken a rule and would have to pay the price. Even telling Elvis she would never cut her hair again didn't calm him down. Priscilla was his woman, and he would have her his way or not at all.

In retrospect, across the decades Priscilla had an epiphany: "The more we were together, the more I came to resemble him in every way. His tastes, his insecurities, his hang-ups, all became mine." Down to his taste in clothes and the color of his hair. His favorite colors were red, blue, turquoise, emerald green, or black and white—these were the colors he wore, and they were the ones he liked to see on Priscilla. She adopted his penchant for high-collared shirts after he told her she needed to cover up her long, skinny neck. Her independence long gone, Priscilla had only one priority in life: "to please [Elvis], to be rewarded with his approval and affection." When she messed up, when his criticism descended on her like a 50-pound weight, she disintegrated. She learned, as the song goes, to "be as tame as a baby or wild as the raging sea," any way he wanted her to be—it was the only way to survive with Elvis.

Obviously, Priscilla did not dare complain about being left in Memphis when Elvis took off for Hollywood or Las Vegas. And when stories of Ann-Margret or Sophia Loren drifted back to Memphis, she just had to suck it up. Once, when she couldn't control herself and asked, "Is it true?" she expected a torrential response. But Elvis replied with a simple, "No." Keogh says Elvis was the model for another famous philanderer, President Bill Clinton, taking the position of deny, deny, deny. It worked both ways—deny Ann-Margret to Priscilla and deny Priscilla to Ann-Margret. Giving up nothing was his refrain, and its melody worked magic most of the time. Elvis may have sung, "I'll be a fool or a wise man," but truth be known he was plenty clever enough to keep all his darlings content with whatever time and love he gave them.

In her effort to compete with the Hollywood stars, Priscilla tried styling like a starlet, with heavy make-up and lofty hairstyles. Elvis decided it was too much after a while and when he said so, Priscilla was crushed. She thought she was doing what he wanted—what he liked in his women. Sometimes she forgot that he loved her *because* she was different. Change was permitted only at his direction, not on her own initiative. She clearly couldn't be "strong as a mountain;" her role was to be "weak as a willow tree," so he could bend her at will.

The more Priscilla complied with Elvis' wishes, the happier her life became. If she let her guard down and missed the mark, perhaps coming down to dinner dressed in a dull color, she caught the brunt of his disappointment. So she learned to dress as he liked, even walk as he instructed (he trained her while watching her walk with a book on her head at Graceland). Sometimes it was tiresome, even exhausting, to stay on her toes all the time. "Would I ever be able to live up to his vision of how his ideal woman should behave and appear?" she pondered on down days. She knew it was a one-way street—his way or the highway—but he could be so loving and generous when he was in the right mood. And even when he wasn't, when he calmed down and his charisma kicked in, he could charm the clothes off her back.

She married him—on May 1, 1967, three weeks before her 22nd birthday, at the Aladdin in Las Vegas. The ceremony wasn't special in the town where marriages could begin and end on a whim, where wedding gowns could be rented or bought off a rack. Priscilla says she had more fittings for dresses she wore to church than she did for her wedding gown. Still, Priscilla was a beautiful bride, a small tiara crowning her pompadour hair covered by a full veil. (Her dress now stands regally in a display case at Graceland—a simple, softly flowing, floor-length gown she designed herself: white silk chiffon with a beaded yoke and sleeves, trimmed in seed pearls.) Elvis, elegantly attired in a black silk brocade tuxedo, sported a platinum watch adorned with sapphires and diamonds, combined with matching cufflinks. A keen observer might have noted that Elvis outshone the bride. At 32, the king sealed his vows to the young girl he had made his own—in spirit, in appearance, and in behavior.

Considering the high profile of the star, the wedding was decidedly low key; it lasted just eight minutes with only a small number of guests. Only a few of the Memphis Mafia were allowed. Joe Esposito was one of the lucky attendees, perhaps because he had loaned Elvis, who never carried cash, the money for the marriage license. Hurt at being left out, some of Elvis' closest associates boycotted a second wedding reception at Graceland on May 29, 1967, for family and friends.

Many of his friends wondered why Elvis gave up his bachelorhood, with producer Hal Kanter pontificating, "Why buy a cow when you can steal the milk through the fence?" Others believe the Colonel instigated the wedding to reduce other influences on Elvis, particularly the spiritual guru Larry Geller.

None of that mattered to Priscilla at the time. Elvis loved her, and he had proved that to the world (including all of his other girls). The 3½-carat diamond ring she wore signified she was the one he loved above all others, and she was his "to take and hold as [he] may."

# 18
# LEAD ME, GUIDE ME

*Lord, just open my eyes that I might see*

~Doris Akers

Away from the formulaic movies that sated many of his fans, Elvis was evolving. Getting married wasn't the only change he was making.

He wanted to move away from the "rocking pop" sound (described by Doll as similar to rock 'n' roll but smooth, effortless, and easy to listen to) that permeated his movies, Elvis evolved into a more dramatic, intense delivery in the next decade. Doll asserts this change was not as revolutionary as Elvis' rockabilly sound of the 50s, but it suited Elvis' personal tastes. In truth, Elvis remained eclectic, adding genres but never totally discarding sounds and styles he liked. Similarly, although he abandoned his flashy dress for sophisticated European-style suits for a while, he later returned to the glitzy style that set him apart on the stage.

Just as his taste in music and clothes was wide-ranging and ever-changing, Elvis had begun exploring new dimensions of spirituality. He had grown up in a simple church where hellfire and brimstone frightened a person into believing. Down the street, he had heard black voices wailing their sorrows and their joys. It was all a part of his life he didn't question. He believed in God, and he sang gospel songs to praise the Lord. But deep in his soul, an unquenchable thirst arose for something more. And then, he heard Larry Geller (an instrument of God, or the devil, some said) speaking, "Draw from this well, it never shall run dry." Like the woman at the well, Elvis eagerly replied, asking the Lord to fill him up and make him whole.

In 1964, Geller had descended into Elvis' life after his regular hairdresser resigned, and the salon (Jay Sebring's — the only men's salon in Los Angeles) recommended Geller as his replacement. As if Elvis sensed spirituality emanating from Geller, on their first meeting, after the haircut, he began, "Larry, let me ask you something...What are you into?"

# MY WAY

Geller had seriously studied spirituality for the previous four years, so he didn't hesitate to respond that although he was a hair stylist by profession, his real interest stemmed from the search for truth—"trying to discover things like where we come from, why we are here, and where we are going."

Elvis grasped Geller like a man reaching for a life preserver. "Man, just keep talking, just keep talking." Elvis lapped up what the spiritualist espoused, dousing his parched soul in new waters of understanding. Geller explained metaphysical and spiritual theories and shared what he had learned from studying Christianity, Hinduism, Buddhism, and Judaism. Elvis, who often struggled with his purpose—why he had been given his talent and how he should use it— listened in awe as Larry revealed he had found his own purpose a couple of years previously: "It's simple. We are given our intelligence, and our life force and our energy, and we're supposed to dedicate our lives to discovering what our mission is and what our purpose is. So, my purpose is to discover my purpose." In response, Elvis told Geller, "'What you're talking about is what I secretly think about all the time...I've always known that there had to be a purpose for my life. I mean there's got to be a reason...why I was chosen to be Elvis Presley.'"

Geller thought his coming to Elvis was preordained. As he told Elvis, "The Hindus have a saying: 'When the pupil is ready, the guru appears.'"

Larry first introduced Elvis to *The Impersonal Life*, a book published in 1917 by Joseph Benner, who proclaimed he was only the conduit for the message—that he hadn't written the message; he was just the instrument transmitting words from a higher power. For Elvis, Brenner's writings opened wide the door he had only been able to wedge. A man who suffered from human weakness, Elvis found comfort and hope in the book's declaration that man's struggles with good and evil are part of the divine plan.

In the book, the divine power discloses, "It is really I, Who causes your personality...to rebel; for your personality with its proud sense of individuality is still needed by Me to develop a mind and body strong enough that they can perfectly express Me..." Moreover, only when a man fully awakens from an earthly life that is nothing more than a dream will "You [Humanity] again become wholly conscious of Me within." Elvis had felt an innate belief that his uniqueness, singing "his way," was a gift, and now his conviction had been affirmed.

Part of Elvis' dream, he relayed to Geller, was an inner voice — in the form of his dead twin — telling him "'to care for other people, to put myself in their place, to see their point of view, to love them.'" He added, "'It was like the voice of conscience.'" The voice of God in *The Impersonal Life* echoed Garon Presley's admonition: "I will cause even you who thus seek to serve me to do many wondrous things towards the quickening and awakening of your brothers." When he read the next lines, Elvis' heart accelerated: "I will cause even you to influence and affect the lives of many of those whom you contact, inspiring and uplifting them to higher ideals." Clearly, Elvis internalized this message; his *How Great Thou Art* album still inspires. And, he not only sang about the love and care of God, he also expressed his desire to serve through his generosity, which ranged from providing funds for a fellow soldier to come home from Germany to be with a dying parent to buying a car for a stranger in a dealership showroom.

His lifelong search for meaning and purpose seemingly finding answers, Elvis invited Geller to join his staff as hairdresser/spiritual adviser. Geller became ever-present, carting in books like *Autobiography of a Yogi, Leaves of Morya's Garden, Beyond the Himalayas, First and Last Freedom*, and scores of other publications touting theories of numerology, cosmology, and metaphysics.

Soon, Larry had become the king's guru — his right hand, and the other guys began to resent the time Elvis spent with him. They made fun of him and looked for ways to make him look like a fool. When Geller joined them at Graceland, they made sure he participated in one of the pick-up football games Elvis always assembled when he was home. An observer might have thought the teams were pros — Elvis outfitted them in regulation helmets and uniforms (their jerseys had patches inscribed with "E.P. ENTP" (Elvis Presley Enterprises) — and indeed Elvis typically turned up a few pro football players to round out his team. Elvis played quarterback and, of course, the king was also the captain of the team. But he couldn't protect his Zen Master. For the Memphis Mafia, payback time had arrived.

A giant of a man, a former Denver Bronco lineman, mowed down Geller on the first play. It was Geller's first and last play; for that game, and any game in the future. In an instant, he went from being a confident Los Angeles hairstylist and spiritualist to a tumbled pile of bones. He returned from the hospital with miles of tape around his broken ribs.

Following Elvis around had its downsides, but it also had benefits, including getting to spend time with the Beatles. Elvis didn't seem overly impressed with the young group from England, who had been eager to meet the king of rock 'n' roll, but the guys hung out together for a while, shooting pool and even jamming a little. His biggest concern, it seems, was whose name—his or the Beatles—was shouted the loudest and the most when they all went out to sign autographs. Geller knew the right answer when Elvis asked—why, Elvis of course, was the name heard above all others. "'Even though there are four of them and one of me...'" Elvis persisted in pondering, never secure in his kingship.

Neither the Colonel nor Priscilla liked Geller any more than the Memphis Mafia did, but he managed to stay around as Elvis' spiritual advisor for longer than any of them wanted. He instructed Elvis, provided him with spiritual readings, and discussed his innermost feelings and needs. But over time, Geller was pushed from the inner circle, and after Priscilla married Elvis, she dropped the books he had given Elvis into an abandoned well at Graceland and set them on fire.

Geller wasn't the only spiritual influence Elvis sought in his journey for inner peace and enlightenment. While filming *Harum Scarum*, he discovered a "Self Realization Fellowship," led by Faye Wright, who had adopted the name of Sri Daya Mata. The fifty-year-old woman, who offered meditation techniques as part of the religious experience, exuded an assurance and serenity that was reminiscent of Elvis' mother. For her part, Daya Mata found "someone full of innocence...a naïve, somewhat childlike individual who was caught up in the adulation of the world and enjoyed it, but more than that, he felt a deep bond with his public; he was carried away by them and didn't want ever to disappoint them...."

Perhaps because of the connection he felt to his mother when he talked with Daya Mata, Elvis opened parts of himself he had left closed even to Geller. No one around him seemed to understand his quest; in fact, the guys resented his spiritual leanings, and he felt cut off from them. As for the Colonel, Elvis was cautious, never forgetting his sense that without the old carny he might not have become king, but Daya Mata detected a subtle pulling back. Intuitively, she recognized the Colonel was pushing Elvis in directions he didn't want to go but felt he should follow because the Colonel had navigated the waters of promotion so successfully. Still, Elvis seemed fretful that "the Colonel did not seem to understand his need to nourish his soul."

Later, Elvis confided in Daya Mata that the constant infighting among his group and the petty politics of moviemaking and recording were sickening, something he had expected the Colonel to keep under control. The more frustrated Elvis became with the caricature of a man he was forced to become by the money-devouring Colonel, the more he turned to Daya Mata. That sealed her fate. The Colonel couldn't afford to have anyone filling Elvis' head with nonsense, especially when it might affect his own influence. Soon, Daya Mata was outlawed. Elvis felt he had lost another soul connection. Someone who understood his calling—"to give back...to awaken in all these young people a closer relationship with God."

Elvis turned back to his Christian roots, finding his yearnings fed by singing religious songs. Interestingly, all three of his Grammy awards recognized his sacred performances and his gospel heritage. Another remarkable aspect of Elvis' career was that, even with rock 'n' roll, R&B, and ballads, his predominant back-up groups were gospel singers: the Jordanaires, the Imperials, the Stamps, and the Statesmen. Filled with the kind of electrical charge Elvis generated himself, the Statesmen featured emotion in their songs, as well as dramatic stage performances not typical of religious groups. They even dressed like they had stepped out of Lansky's on Beale Street. Elvis saw something of himself, too, in the ceaseless jiggling of bass singer Jim Wetherington's legs. Jake Hess, the Statesmen's lead singer, says Wetherington "went about as far as you could go in gospel music...the women would jump up, just like they do for the pop shows." Preachers complained about the lewd movements, and civil rights activists objected to the theft of style from Negro spirituals.

Elvis' female vocal group, the Sweet Inspirations, gave him a bit of space from such criticism, since they were black. And, unlike some of the other groups, they sang other genre, too, as well as gospel.

When Elvis had moved to Memphis with his parents in 1948, the town was hopping with music—from delta blues to rockabilly to Southern gospel. Elvis was too young to go down Beale Street in his early days in the city, so he turned to the monthly all-night gospel sings at Ellis Auditorium. At first, he was just one face among the 5,000 who clapped and stomped their feet to the gospel sounds of groups like the Blackwood Brothers and the Statesmen. These men were superstars to Elvis, and in time he worked up enough courage to introduce himself to them.

It was at Ellis Auditorium that Elvis first met J.D. Sumner, the founder of the Stamps. Later, when Sumner recalled not seeing Elvis in the audience a couple of times, since Elvis was usually there, the next time he saw him he asked why he had been missing in the monthly audience. Elvis told him he sometimes didn't have money for a ticket, so Sumner solved that problem in a heartbeat: From that time forward, he let Elvis in the back door. And Elvis rarely missed the annual National Quartet Convention in Memphis, which Sumner had started. From just a nobody in the audience, unnoticed by those surrounding him, one of the Imperials says that, after his stardom, "When [Elvis] walked in, it was like royalty in the room."

Elvis recorded his first gospel album after he returned from the Army, and a video of him singing "His Hand in Mine," which made the *Billboard* chart, shows sadness behind his smile. The words about doubt are tinged with melancholy, and even though he sings, "I'll never walk alone...he will guide each step I take," with soulfulness, one feels his uncertainty. "I can feel his hand in mine, that's all I need to know" sounds hollow, as if he doesn't really *know*. He is still searching, and the one place where he might feel God's presence is off limits—his presence in church disrupted the service. So he brought religion to his home. Gathering quartets at Graceland to sing formed his private worship service. He also watched televangelists, especially Rex Humbard. By singing gospel and then listening to Humbard, Elvis felt he had worshipped in "his way." It was as if he had been to the chapel, "where people are of one accord...just to sing and praise the Lord."

Having grown up in a Pentecostal church, Elvis threw himself into gospel music with fervor, but he often told some of the quartet members he never felt worthy. He constantly asked the question, "How will I know when I have the Holy Spirit?" He once said, "I just want what my mama had; she had something really good." He read the Bible regularly, and he believed it, yet he felt empty most of the time. Despite his doubts, he saw helping others as his mission. Myrna Smith, a member of the Sweet Inspirations, recalls Elvis' concern when one of the singing group was diagnosed with cancer. "Elvis touched Sylvia's stomach and prayed for God to take the cancer." Astonishingly, she relates, the next morning tests showed Sylvia' cancer was gone.

Myrna also recollects that racial tension was at an all-time high when the Sweet Inspirations began singing with Elvis. Before one concert in Texas, Elvis was told to "leave the black girls at home." But Elvis stood up for his back-up musicians, refusing to do the show without them. And, Myrna notes, he always treated them not only with respect but also as equals. If others didn't like it, she said, Elvis' attitude was, "Deal with it." And he wasn't making a political statement. He had grown up near blacks, and they were as good as he was.

When Elvis sang, "If I can dream of a better land," the Sweet Inspirations knew he truly wanted a land "where my brothers can walk hand in hand" as much as they did. Today, watching a DVD of Elvis singing "There must be peace and understanding sometime," there is no doubt the words came from his heart. He knew what it was like to be "trapped in a world that's troubled with pain," and his yearning to "redeem his soul and fly" grips listeners' heartstrings. The pain and abject misery in his face, the passion and desire in his voice, take one deep into his soul and were it not for the ending of the song, that a beckoning candle persuades him not to give up hope, to keep dreaming, the song would be tragic instead of uplifting.

Guralnick notes that although Elvis loved all types of music, gospel grounded him. Quartet music united Elvis' deep spirituality, which he sensed in all types of music, with the exodus he constantly sought—the escape from earthly doubts and frustrations. It was in gospel music that Elvis' inner being came close to "slip[ping] the surly bounds of earth to touch the face of God."

RCA didn't particularly like Elvis' recording gospel, but when Elvis put his foot down about something he wanted to do, most people knew to give in or face unpleasant consequences. When he decided to record his second gospel album, Ray Walker of the Jordanaires suggested "How Great Thou Art." Elvis had never heard of the song, but when he listened to the words, he knew how he wanted to sing it—with a big choir sound. That was a bit much for RCA, but he cajoled them into using both the Jordanaires and the Imperials, along with a couple of female singers, to get the sound he wanted. Walker believes, "How Great Thou Art" was Elvis' personal praise, adding, "You could see his soul."

Even during his days as a film star, Elvis had the guts to do gospel on the side. He never wondered, "What will all the young girls think?" Part of his purpose, he felt, was to turn them—and indeed the world—on to gospel music. Initially, for the most part, he stuck with oldies like "If It Wasn't for the Lighthouse," his head shaking in disbelief, stoked with a sense that he was in the lighthouse as he sang, near enough to touch his savior.

Had he lived longer, Elvis might have become one of the first contemporary Christian singers. One of his favorite religious songs was "Sweet, Sweet Spirit," and he once had a quartet sing it in a shower stall so he could hear the reverberations. Watching a video of him in a studio when the song is being recorded, one is surprised he isn't singing. His face pale, eyes closed, Elvis' head turns downward in a thoughtful pose of prayer. Then, he looks up and smiles, a touch of heaven shimmering in his eyes before he looks down again, feeling the music. He mouths the words silently, sometimes as sweat trickles down his face. When the song concludes, with a crooked smile, a small "Whew…" escapes from his lips.

The messages of gospel songs touched Elvis' heart just as love ballads did. If the ballads gave words to pining for love, the gospel songs gave expression to the troubled questions for which he couldn't find answers. "When the storms of life are raging, stand by me" echoed his need for solace in a world clamoring for him.

Over the years, Elvis grew increasingly uncomfortable with the adulation afforded him. At a Notre Dame concert, when a group of girls in the center of the auditorium unfurled a banner with the words, "Elvis,

You're the King," Elvis looked at it for a moment and then signaled silence. "No," he said quietly but fervently, "Jesus Christ is the King."

He believed his success, and the worldly possessions it allowed, came from God. Perhaps that's why another of his most beloved songs was "He Touched Me." J.D. Sumner's daughter once said Elvis listened to the Gaithers' recording of this song more than 50 times. She also shared that her father thought Elvis always wanted to be a gospel singer but destiny had something else in mind for him. Jake Hess agreed, noting Elvis himself had said he would have liked to devote his life to singing gospel, but he couldn't; he had too many people depending on him.

Elvis also told J.D. Sumner he wanted to be a bass singer, just like him, but "God messed up." Horsing around one day, when J.D. went to the bottom of the bass well at the end of "Bosom of Abraham," Elvis playfully put both of his hands on J.D.'s head and pushed him backward.

Elvis was close to several members of his gospel quartets, but J.D. held a special place of honor in his heart. When he heard the Stamps needed a new tour bus, Elvis called J.D. to his room and handed him a check, staying, "Make this out for your bus, J.D." Astounded, J.D. said, "I can't make it out—this is your check." Quick on the draw, Elvis responded, "You can write, can't you?" After a bit more persuasion, J.D. accepted the check. About that time Elvis added one caveat: "Only thing—when you get the bus, bring it to Memphis and let me drive it." And that's exactly what J.D. did, almost causing Elvis to decide, "This time, Lord, You gave me a mountain, a mountain I may never climb," when he got behind the wheel. He did okay until he realized he didn't know how to put the bus in reverse. The Lord let him off the mountain and told him to just keep going...through a big field. J.D. later said he was thinking as they bounced through the ruts in the corn field, "There goes my new bus...." But Elvis made it back safely to Graceland, telling J.D. "Well, you kept your word." J.D. answered, "Yes, so did you."

For all of his life, Elvis remained an ardent fan of black gospel and Southern white gospel, but he also embraced the contemporary music coming from the west coast. The Imperials brought him the new genre, and as he had done all of his life, he relished something different. For

133

Elvis to pick up a song, one of the Imperials once noted, "It had to be something directly related to his life...." He could express his emotions in songs like "I Believe" or "A Thing Called Love" as easily as he could in more traditional gospel songs. There was a message there, too. He could identify with, "Some men are like me, they worry and doubt, trouble their minds day in and day out." And just as "He Touched Me" spoke to his heart, so did a song about love that you couldn't see with your eyes or hold in your hands—a love that could rule the heart of any man, lifting him up, putting him down, taking his world and turning it around. He had no doubt: "Ever since time nothing's ever been found, stronger than love" because he knew it was God who blessed the world "with a thing called love."

Elvis' long search for spirituality carried him on journeys through other religions. His quest to become what God wanted him to be led him far and wide, but in the end, he found that while he was more educated after having read books like *The Impersonal Life*, it was in the Bible he found peace and joy. J. D. shared that he and Elvis often read the Bible and prayed in the early hours of the morning after everyone else had left for bed.

Rex Humbard also has memories of time spent with Elvis, talking about the Bible. He recalls Elvis was struck when Humbard's wife told the story of a "bell sheep." In the holy land, there is one sheep who has a bell; when he moves, the rest follow. Rex's wife says as she told Elvis, "I'm praying you are the bell sheep that will lead people to Christ," Elvis began to tremble and weep. Once again, he was "crying in the chapel, where humble people go to pray." He prayed to the Lord he would "grow stronger as [he] lived from day to day." But the burden weighed heavily on his shoulders.

# 19
# GOT A LOT O' LIVING TO DO

*Oh yes I've got a lot o' living to do*

*A whole lot o' loving to do*

~Aaron Schroeder and Ben Weisman

Elvis had the whole world at his feet—fans who idolized him, a wife who worshipped him, and enough money to buy anything he wanted. His latest fancy was horses. He had bought one for Priscilla before they married, and soon everybody had a horse. A riding ring was built, and the barn, which Elvis dubbed "House of the Rising Sun," was fixed up, with the names of the horses inscribed on their stalls with a red marker pen. The temporary respite helped, but Elvis soon had to return to the real world where the Colonel was working on deals—this time for himself.

After all, the Colonel told Elvis, he was devoting his life to the star. He had no other clients, so he hitched his wagon a little higher in the sky, marking off more of the star for himself. On existing contracts, the Colonel would continue his 25-percent take on flat fees as a management payment, but on profits—what Elvis earned beyond the flat fees—his cut would increase to 50 percent. It was a sweetheart deal considering the royalties from Elvis' records and his films. (The deal for merchandising had always been 50-50 since the Colonel was the one who did all the work and Elvis only contributed his name and image.) Although the deal may not have been shocking—or even unprecedented—in the music industry, it galled Vernon Presley, who knew the Colonel was outwitting them in ways the new 50-50 split would never reveal. But Elvis never suspected the Colonel would soon be renegotiating old contracts to significantly reduce the old guaranteed payment schedule, thus benefitting the Colonel and taking money from Elvis' pocket. As far as Elvis was concerned, there was plenty of money to go around. Right now, he was spending a large portion of his share on stallions.

Soon, Elvis had bought a 160-acre farm in Mississippi to house his growing herd of horses. He bought the place lock, stock, and barrel — cattle, house, furnishings, about everything except the owner's clothes. Even in the mid-60s, it was a hefty purchase: $437,000 (more than $2.8 million in 2011.) And that was just the beginning. Naturally, all the horses he would be buying required more fencing, to the tune of $12,000 ($77,000 in 2011.) Overnight, in addition to the commitment to buy the farm, he had shelled out more than $100,000 ($646,000 in 2011). With the Colonel now taking a larger share of profits, Vernon began to fear Elvis was going to buy them back into the poorhouse. Elvis was chasing the "ghost rider in the sky."

It was as close to heaven as Elvis had been in a long time. He felt rejuvenated, getting up earlier than he had in years. He was ready to make up for all of the lost time working so hard — he had a "whole lot of living to do...and there [was] no one [he'd] rather do it with than [his little Cilla]." In Priscilla's words, "He was having a ball," adding that some days he didn't take time to come to the farmhouse to eat. "He'd walk around with a loaf of bread under his arm in case hunger pangs struck." Days were spent riding, skeet shooting, and having picnics. It was so much fun Elvis decided each of the Memphis Mafia should own a piece of the action, and it took Vernon's forceful voice to stop Elvis from deeding over an acre to each of them.

Even without part ownership in the farm, the guys enjoyed their time there. Jerry Shilling recalls how peaceful it was as he sat in his little trailer by the lake, enjoying down time with his wife. "It was really beautiful at first," he recalled. "You'd wake up in the morning, the horses would be drinking out of the lake; Elvis and Priscilla would ride over, and we'd go for a ride, then have breakfast."

But it was too good to last. After the fun of buying things died down, Elvis seemed kind of glum. Even with Priscilla at his side and his friends close by, loneliness seeped in. Elvis began to feel poorly, and shortly afterward, he began to gain weight. By the time he was due to depart for his next film, he had to beg for more time. The Colonel demanded a doctor's certificate, but Elvis' regular doctor wasn't available. At the suggestion of George Klein's girlfriend, who worked for a doctors' group, he engaged Dr. George Nichopoulos.

# GOT A LOT O' LIVING TO DO

After several days under the care of "Dr. Nick," Elvis thought he felt well enough to travel to California to begin filming. He was still wobbly, though, and fell the first night he was there, suffering a minor concussion. Enough was enough. The Colonel took charge and read everyone the riot act. They were on payroll to take care of Elvis, and they had let him down. About all that accomplished was to increase infighting.

Priscilla had her own set of problems. She was pregnant and didn't want to be. She had begged Elvis to let her take birth control pills when they married, but he vetoed that, saying he wasn't sure they were safe. Priscilla was beginning to chafe at the ironclad control Elvis had over her, and she resented having to spend the first year of her marriage preparing for a child instead of living the good life while traveling with Elvis. On his end, life would go on as usual, although he announced, "This is the greatest thing that has ever happened to me." Now he *really* had a lot o' living to do.

It was good Elvis had something to excite him, because business was bad — so bad his latest movie, *Easy Come, Easy Go*, hadn't brought in enough ticket sales to cover costs. Even the accompanying sound track felt dismally short of projections with sales not even reaching 40,000. Although there were three movies remaining on the MGM contract, no one seemed anxious to move ahead with them, and for sure no one was offering new contracts.

The young rebel was adrift as America seethed over another generational shift; race, war and politics had grabbed our attention. Elvis' movies, and his music seemed out of touch.

Cutbacks had to be made, Vernon declared, and the horse ranch was one of the victims. Out-go was exceeding income, and even Elvis realized changes had to be made, not only in the way he was spending money but also in the way he was earning it. He had heard a new song by another RCA singer, Jerry Reed, and he thought it might be a good fit for him. The song, "Guitar Man," embellished with Reed's forceful acoustic sound, was hard to duplicate, though, until someone realized that the guitar-playing men in the studio were using picks, while Reed used his own fingers to pound the strings. Elvis realized Reed was the key, and he sent for him to join the session. When the "Alabama Wild

Man" arrived, magic materialized. The new sound was both as soft as a rock skimming over water and as driving as a summer storm. Almost like a shimmer of moonlight on a rough ocean.

Reed remembers the session well, admitting he thought he would be nervous playing with Elvis. "I got pumped, and then Elvis got pumped, and the more he got pumped up, the more I did — it was like a snowball effect." He adds that he was on cloud nine. "Once Elvis got the spirit, things really began to happen. When the guitars and the rhythm sounded right, I guess the guitar lick kind of reminded him of 'What'd I Say,' and he just sort of started testifying at the end. That was how it happened — one of those rare moments in your life you never forget."

Elvis was coming back. After his record producer, Felton Jarvis, suggested Elvis sound mad, even mean, Elvis' voice became rough as they moved on to "Big Boss Man." He felt invigorated and motivated again.

With Elvis' last movie a lackluster success at the box office, the Colonel looked to special radio shows for income, then turned his efforts toward a 1968 Christmas special on NBC. Adroitly, he tacked on a motion picture, bringing the upfront money to more than a million dollars. Priscilla knew how she wanted to spend some of that — she found a house sitting high on a hill overlooking Los Angeles — a home away from home. Thankfully, it wasn't large enough for the entire Mafia to live with them, and she hoped at last they could begin life as a family. Having a home in California would enable her and the baby to be wherever Elvis was. A few months later, Elvis shocked her by saying he wanted a trial separation. Time apart would help both of them, he insisted. Priscilla was at a loss to understand what brought this sudden revelation on, especially when their child would be born soon. Strangely, after the one conversation, Elvis never brought up the topic again. Priscilla didn't dare ask questions, but she tried to explain to herself. "Elvis would do things like that when he didn't feel worthy, or he felt that he'd been bad and he didn't want to hurt me. He seemed to feel better after he said it. He had so many ups and downs; life would basically interfere with his emotions, sometimes on a daily basis."

Over the years, Priscilla became accustomed to Elvis' moods, knowing that when someone upset him, even his father, he would disappear upstairs and not come down for several days. "He had a difficult time confronting his emotions, confronting conflicts," she said, noting if you left him alone, he would eventually come out of it.

Still young, Priscilla gained wisdom beyond her years, fathoming, "You went with the ride... One thing that I realized was that he loved the chase. And once the chase was over, I knew I didn't have to worry about anything—whether it was a new game or a girl... He would always come home." She adds that once she realized that about Elvis, she grasped that "it was just a matter of time; it just depended on how long he wanted to play the game, and whether you wanted to wait." Elvis still had a lot o' living to do, and for now, Priscilla wanted to be part of it.

# 20

# ONE NIGHT WITH YOU

*One night with you*

*is what I'm now praying for*

~Dave Bartholomew, Pearl King, and Anita Steimer

Elvis' mood swings affected everybody around him. For years, he had hidden his erratic personality from everyone except those closest to him. Now, even in recording sessions, he behaved oddly out of character. Ray Walker, one of the Jordanaires who had worked with him since 1958, observed he had never heard Elvis use profanity, but in a Nashville recording session, "...things got jokingly rough; there was some language going on." The session lasted four hours, and by the time it ended, all of the musicians escaped gladly, some offended by Elvis' attacks on them and others relieved they had eluded his sharp temper.

Priscilla knew she wasn't the only one catching the brunt of Elvis' up and down disposition. She feared the cause originated from his "constant intake of 'medication,'" but she dared not suggest he cut back on the pills. And, she couldn't do anything about the other source of his frustration—the Colonel. Increasingly, Elvis believed the Colonel was "'messing with his music.'" It had started with the forced inclusion of inappropriate and silly songs in the movies. Now, his obsession on profit had kept "Guitar Man" from coming out as a single because of a disagreement on the rights to the song. He even began to suspect the Colonel had someone tamper with the tapes after he left the recording studio. The songs just didn't sound the same on the records as they did in the studio. While the Colonel deserved some of the criticism Elvis had begun to heap on his head (in absentia, of course), Elvis' thinking had become almost delusional. The lack of success on the charts and at the box office made him paranoid.

The upside of Elvis' state of mind was that he stayed at home more, especially since the birth of Lisa Marie—when she arrived, Elvis announced he was the happiest man in the world; and, for a time, he was. Staring at the tiny baby girl in her crib, his heart soared with pride. His only regret was that his mother had not lived to see her granddaughter.

His love for his daughter unquestionable, Elvis turned from the mother of his child, especially in the bedroom. He no longer desired even "one night" with her. Priscilla read his refusal to make love with her after Lisa Marie's birth as rejection. Elvis, who had put her on such a pedestal he wouldn't have sex with her until after marriage, had lost all physical attraction for her. Devastated, Priscilla shared her frustration and shame only with her diary. "It's been two months, and he still hasn't touched me. I'm getting concerned." In a later entry, she wrote she had embarrassed herself. "I wore a black negligee, laid as close to Elvis as I could while he read. I guess it was because I knew what I wanted and was making it obvious. I kissed his hand, then each finger, then his neck and face. But I waited too long. His sleeping pills had taken effect." She concluded the entry with, "Another lonely night."

Trying to unravel the problem, Priscilla recalled Elvis had told her before they were married that he had never been able to make love with a woman who had had a child. At the time, she never suspected the hang-up would extend to her.

Desperate for affection, Priscilla had an affair with her dance teacher. Elvis wouldn't call her to his side, and she had been lonely too long. Punishing Elvis in this way was heresy. Men could do whatever they wanted, but women had their prescribed place and behavior in Elvis' world.

Although others suspected what was going on, to Elvis it was simply inconceivable—Priscilla belonged to him. Besides, he had his mind on the upcoming Christmas special. For once, he had overruled the Colonel, who wanted Elvis to sing Christmas songs, in keeping with the season. One hour of Christmas music was absurd, Elvis declared, and he wasn't going to do it. The Colonel backed down and acquiesced to Elvis' demand that he wanted the show to be as unlike the music of his movies as possible. In fact, he wanted it to be different from anything he had ever done. The show's producer, Bob Finkel, recalls Elvis made it clear he was "not interested in what Colonel Parker has to say about this show," adding Elvis wanted everyone to know "what he can really do." And that, the audio engineer who had worked with him back in the old days declared, would require the same emotional commitment he had made to his early records. By then, the show's director, Steve Binder, was on board. He had been reticent to work with Elvis — he wasn't really a fan — but now he sensed the excitement of creating a show that would remind people who Elvis Presley was. "It would all stem from *his* life, *his* music, *his* experience."

Binder's idea was to use a play called "Blue Bird" as the theme around which the show would be built. In the story, the main character searches for fame and fortune but finds the only true happiness is back home. Jerry Reed's "Guitar Man" would form the central musical theme. Although apprehensive that Elvis might not be turned on by the idea, Binder found Elvis enthusiastic when he presented the plan. What Elvis needed was one night with the only true love in his life — his audience — and with Binder's plan he could reach them. They could make his dreams come true again, just as they had done before.

After a Hawaiian holiday with Priscilla, which he thought might help the faltering relationship; Elvis came back fit and trim. For the first time in years, he was anxious to get back to work, excited at the possibility of a show that would be genuine Elvis — not a caricature created by the Colonel and the movie producers. He was engaged and motivated, and the only downers were the assassinations — only two months apart — of Martin Luther King and Bobby Kennedy. Listening to Elvis bemoan the loss of two men he respected, men who advanced the cause of civil rights just as Elvis did, albeit in a different way, Binder knew he wanted America to feel what Elvis felt about the tragic tension between two races.

Looking back, Binder explains it this way: "I wanted to let the world know that here was a guy who was not prejudiced, who was raised in the heart of prejudice, but who was above all that. Part of the strength that I wanted to bring to the show was that sense of compassion, that this was somebody to look up to and admire."

Elvis was back to his old self — caring, concerned, respectful. The temper tantrums had receded into a dark corner of his mind and couldn't find their way out in the excitement he was feeling about singing "his way." Cheerful and upbeat, he inspired everyone around him with his work ethic and willingness to make the show the best of the season. Anticipating one night with his audience gave him an adrenalin rush.

Billy Goldenberg worked with Elvis to perfect his performance with one goal in mind: He wanted Elvis to show who he was beneath the clothes and the sulky smile. "I wanted to tune in to Elvis underneath. I wanted to tune in to the perversity, frankly, that was deep inside him...to the darkness, to the wild, untamed, animalistic things." Yes, Elvis could be sweet and kind, but he wouldn't reveal himself by syrupiness. "He was blatantly sexual, and that was something I wanted in the music. And if I could get that, I felt I was getting closer to the raw Elvis."

It didn't take him long to get there. In the first rehearsal, when Elvis finished "Guitar Man," he was on such "a high...so involved and excited and emotionally charged...it was like he had fornicated," Billy says. If "Guitar Man" opened the show on that high note, how on earth could they match it in the finale of the show? The Colonel, who had lost the battle for having an hour of Christmas songs, was still trying to win the war by having the last song be seasonal. But Steve knew what he wanted; he just couldn't find it. The one thing he knew for sure was that it wasn't "I'll Be Home for Christmas." Finally, he asked Earl Brown, a vocal arranger, to write a song that would put an exclamation mark on the show. The next morning Earl played the song he had written overnight, "If I Can Dream."

"That's it," Steve proclaimed. "You've just written the song that's going to close the show."

As he often did when he connected with a song, Elvis didn't just listen to Brown play the song once. He asked him to play it over and over, maybe as many as eight times. With Steve and Brown thinking Elvis must not like the song, Elvis finally looked up and said, "We're doing it."

Brown had written the lyrics, but they were Elvis' words. Guralnick describes how Elvis made it his own, explaining it is not the poignancy of the message about the brotherhood of all men—the craving for peace and universal understanding— that grabs and captivates listeners, then and now, but the rawness of emotion in Elvis' voice that has staying power.

The song echoed King's famous "I have a dream" speech, and Elvis poured his heart into it. Alone on the stage, he asked Binder to dim the lights for the final take.

"I think he was oblivious to everything else in the universe. When I looked out the window, he was in an almost fetal position, writhing on the cement floor, singing that song." In the live television show later, standing alone, almost messianic in a white double-breasted suit, Elvis' right hand swung like a pendulum as he unleashed inner turmoil, almost shouting the song's final lines, "Let the dream come true, right now."

"And," Binder recalls, "when he got done, he came in the control room, and we played it maybe fifteen times, he just loved it so much." That night, Keogh says Elvis showed he could still galvanize listeners — his power to connect and convey the depths of his being had not been lost. He could still tear the roof off, she declares, "with rough-hewn versions of songs...."

The television show itself brought a metamorphosis in Elvis. First, part of the show had been taped in front of a live audience — the place where Elvis felt most at ease. And, the stunning black leather suit designed by Bill Belew was the perfect costume for the tanned, feral man who said he was doing the show "because we figure the time is right and today's music is right." With his trademark curled lip smile, he added, "Also, I thought I might ought to do this special before I get too old."

The Elvis who once caused fans to faint when they saw him on the big screen now viewed him close up on their television screens. Steve had taken a risk, going against the odds by looking for the man beneath the movie mask, and without a doubt, he says, "...everything that everyone objected to — the sweat, the hair falling down his face — that was the blood and guts of the show, that was what people liked." At the end of the show, Elvis sent for the Colonel. "I want to tour again. I want to go out and work with a live audience." He was done, he declared, "with...movies. I've had a smash TV special. I'm ready to cut some records." The comeback kid had had his one night with his fans, and he wanted more to make his dreams come true.

Elvis didn't need to wait for the show to air to know he had found himself again. Before 42 percent of the viewing public made the show number one for the season and gave NBC its highest ratings of the year, Elvis knew. One night with his fans had been all he needed.

In charge of his own future for the first time, he recorded some of his best records and had some of his best stage performances.

Las Vegas, the king is coming.

# Chapter 21
# IT'S NOW OR NEVER

*Tomorrow will be too late*

*It's now or never*

~Eduardo Di Capua, Aaron Schroeder, and Wally Gold

Peter Guralnick, in his 1968 *Boston Phoenix* review of the NBC special, used Elvis' own words to kick off his article: "It's been a long time, baby." Mesmerized by Elvis' performance, he wrote that it took only minutes for Elvis to shed the lethargy shadowing his return from the army. Suddenly, the blandness faded as he regained his surly sense of defiance. The wildness that wired and super-charged his fans returned in fury, and one only had to look at the sweat pouring down his face to know the old Elvis had been reincarnated. Thirty years later, Guralnick still remembered his personal reaction and recorded it in his book, *Careless Love*, calling Elvis' appearance a resurrection, saying it was nothing like he had ever seen or experienced on television. Finding it difficult to convey the excitement of the moment, he describes it as "both a revelation and a vindication."

The king was back! And he was returning to the one place he had failed miserably 13 years previously. Risky, but that was "his way." It was going to be his first live appearance in eight years, and he would depend on his well-hewn instincts. In Vegas, he was placing the biggest bet of his life. Two live shows a night in a town where, in 1956, for the first time in his life, he hadn't been able to connect with an audience. The memory of that miserable night stubbornly stayed in his mind over the years—people sitting quietly while he sang his heart out, their faces carved in stone. The only way to mask the memory was to return to the scene where he had bombed. After the dismal response to his movies recently, Vegas was a dicey choice for a comeback. But for Elvis, it was now or never.

The gamble paid off. At the International Hotel, between July 31,

# IT'S NOW OR NEVER

1969 and August 31, 1969, Elvis headlined 57 shows, consistently packing a 2,000-capacity room while the icons of Vegas, Frank Sinatra and Dean Martin, sang to a paltry 1200.

Elvis didn't merely roll the dice on his performance; he took a deck of cards and studied every one, ready to play his hand when the first night of his Vegas gig began. He was the ace, but he needed some jacks and even a king or two, and he went through a bevy of musicians in search of the winning hand. He finally turned to someone he had never met but admired, James Burton, who had played with Ricky Nelson; and after talking on the phone for two hours, Burton agreed to put a band together. In addition to Burton, the group included rhythm guitarist John Wilkinson, Memphis pianist Larry Muhoberac, and bass player Jerry Scheff. The vocal groups included the Imperials, who had qualms about going to Vegas since they were gospel singers, and the Sweet Inspirations, who had previously backed up Aretha Franklin. Elvis handpicked these two groups with the goal of combining black gospel harmony with a white quartet sound, creating a continuum of sounds that would integrate American music in a way it had not been done before.

The Sweet Inspirations, who had never met Elvis, also had concerns. Elvis erased their anxiety in a heartbeat when he walked in and started singing a song from their record. When their voices joined his, they bonded. Myrna Smith later said Elvis added the Sweet Inspirations "because he wanted the spice of soul...." Looking back, she recalls the Vegas show as the most exciting show she ever worked. And she had worked not only with Aretha but also Tom Jones, and other stars. The excitement stemmed, she said, from Elvis' love of singing and performing. "I mean, Aretha could sing rings around Elvis if you're talking about vocal prowess, but as far as wanting to be on that stage, I mean, you just got drawn into it."

Rehearsing with Elvis for the opening night was a roller coaster ride. He would be at the top of the ride, exhilarated as he anticipated a spectacular comeback, but he descended the hill more than once into utter panic that he would fall on his face. Sometimes he was on the "now" and sometimes he hit the "never."

Elvis, desperate for reassurance, called his old friend, Sam Phillips,

147

to come to Vegas to critique the performance. His review was simple and began with a question: "Is the goddamn rhythm section kicking you in the ass? Where is the placement of the rhythm section...Just put the rhythm out there baby, just put it out there. That is your I-den-ti-fi-cation." Later, Sam found his advice had been heeded. "When I saw the show I want to tell you, I *never* heard a better rhythm section in my life. There was some randy ass shit. I told him that."

Elvis did reject one piece of advice from Sam—to delete "Memories" from the show's program. Like the other songs on the program, "Memories" spoke to Elvis, and he wasn't going to cut the groovy song.

When the big moment arrived, the late July night hung hot and heavy over the city, but Elvis didn't need the heat to make him perspire. He was so nervous he couldn't stand still, and Joe Esposito says sweat poured from him before he went onstage. But when he walked out, it was "now."

In the audience, the list of celebrities read like a page from "Who's Who": Pat Boone, Fats Domino (who Elvis once said was the real king of rock 'n' roll), Cary Grant, Wayne Newton, Ann-Margret, Dick Clark, George Hamilton, Petula Clark, and Henry Mancini, among others.

In front of this lustrous gathering, Elvis strode on stage with no introduction. As the audience sat silent and still in anticipation, Elvis grabbed the microphone, curved his body into the stance that had made him famous, and jiggled his leg. The crowd went wild. Elvis was back, and this time Vegas loved him.

Clad in a mock karate suite of black mohair, Elvis looked like a gorgeous King Kong. Before he opened his mouth in song, the crowd roared, giving him a standing ovation. Then Elvis rocked with "Blue Suede Shoes," detonating the crowd like a bomb as he moved into "I Got A Woman" and "All Shook Up." In the midst of the explosion, be began crooning, "Love Me Tender," and the blasts that had shattered the room gave way to swoons. Before the ladies could faint, Elvis burst into a medley of "Don't Be Cruel" and "Jailhouse Rock." Elvis had the women—and the men—in the palm of his hand. They might be dressed more sedately than Elvis and the Sweets (the audience elegant in evening gowns and tuxedos), but they felt the same raw emotion teenagers had experienced a decade before. And when he stepped off the edge of the stage, leaned over, and kissed a few of the surprised but ecstatic ladies, it's surprising medics didn't have to be called for the swooning recipients of the full, on-the-mouth smackers.

"Suspicious Minds," which the audience hadn't heard previously but eventually became Elvis' first number-one single since 1962, brought on a second standing ovation before Elvis put the crowd on their feet again as he closed with "What'd I Say." When the crowd wouldn't stop their cries for more, Elvis came back for an encore, singing "Can't Help Falling in Love." It created such a powerful ending it became the song Elvis used to close every show for the rest of his singing career.

From animalistic to crooning, Elvis enchanted and hypnotized everyone in the room the night he made his comeback. Doll believes Elvis changed Vegas venues—from "smooth pop crooners" to a new crop of singers producing music with a "rock-influenced sound" that was grander both in glitz and sex appeal. Tom Jones and Engelbert Humperdinck saw how Elvis' style captivated audiences, and they adapted their own performances, as did many others. Humperdinck acknowledged Elvis' influence: "I learned about humility, charm, and how to work an audience from watching Elvis in concert. If you're going to steal—and every performer does it from someone at some time—then steal from the best, which was Elvis." Whatever he did to influence future Vegas shows—his and others—Elvis' fans left no doubt how they felt about the man who touched their heart and imagination with his voice.

The reviews matched the audience's reaction. The *New Yorker* applauded "Presley's sustaining love for rhythm and blues, while the British *Record Mirror* depicted Elvis as a "wild beast, roaring through a long list of the songs that made him famous," adding that "ladies lost years and threw themselves at the feet of their leader in frenzied glory." Even the *Hollywood Reporter*, a long-time critic, had a difficult time saying anything bad about the performance. The *New York Times*, in its feature, "A White Boy with Black Hips," had to admit what some had sneered at in the past had mesmerized old and young alike.

The more comfortable Elvis got on the stage, the more he played around. Almost every night this included telling the audience he had been studying to be an electrician when he accidentally ended up in show business. "...I was wired the wrong way. One day on my lunch break I went to make a little demonstration record—I mean, I really wasn't trying to get into the business, but about a year and a half later the guy put the record out. No one had heard of me, but just overnight people were saying, 'Is He? Is He?' and I'm going, 'Am I? Am I?' I became pretty big in my hometown and a few parts of the country, and I started working nightclubs and football fields, little weird rooms where people were going, 'Hmm, hmm,' you know, and they threw me off the *Opry*, and Arthur Godfrey took one look and said, 'Nah, nah,' so I did that for a year and a half and then I met Colonel Sanders—Parker.

"So I went to New York, and people were saying, 'Get him, get him, hot damn, he's just out of the trees'...So there was a lot of controversy, and I went on the *Ed Sullivan Show*." As Elvis tells about the cameras filming him from the waist up, the crowd roars. Then he rolls into the time the producers of the *Steve Allen Show* dressed him in a tuxedo and made him sing to a dog on a stool. "The dog is peeing, and I didn't know it, you know, so I'm singing, 'You ain't nothing but a hound dog,' and the dog's going, 'Ump, ump,' and I'm going, 'Back, back, you fool,' and the dog ran out of the room."

When the laughter died down, Elvis talked a bit about his Hollywood days, saying he was living it up pretty good until "I got drafted, shafted, and everything else. Just overnight it was all gone, you know. I was in a different world, and I woke up, and it was gone."

In the service, Elvis related that the guys "must get awful lonesome, because they call each other 'mother' a lot." Laugher bounced off the walls before Elvis got serious, saying after his return he concentrated on movies but found "as the years went by it got harder and harder to perform to a movie camera, and I really missed the people. I really missed contact with a live audience. And I just wanted to tell you how good it is to be back."

Spellbound, the audience sat silently for a split second, and then a roar built to a crescendo. With candor and charm, Elvis had shared his journey, and the response validated that "his way" was the right way.

Priscilla has her own memories of the opening night. As usual, Elvis had supervised the selection of her attire—white go-go boots anchoring a white-fringed mini-dress that bared her midriff. But that's not what she treasures. Elvis' energy enveloped the stage and the audience, his charisma captivating everyone in the huge room, drawing them in as if Elvis was personally singing to them. "I don't think I've ever felt that [such charisma] in any entertainer since. I mean, yes, other entertainers have charisma, but Elvis exuded a maleness about him, a proudness that you would see in an animal. On the stage he'd have this look, you know, prowling back and forth, pacing like a tiger, and you look and you say, 'My god, is this the person that I…?' It was difficult to attach who he was to this person on stage. It was incredible."

Like Priscilla, Elvis' hairdresser (Patti Parry) saw a man she thought she knew well, since she had been with him eight years; but he went through a metamorphosis on the stage, like a light shined on him and the electricity from Elvis and from the audience transformed him into a wild but delectable creature.

Everyone there felt the magnetism. Felton, the show's producer, recalls Elvis was all over the stage, "doing flips and cartwheels and all kinds of stuff; on 'Suspicious Minds' he'd be down on one knee and do a flip across stage and just roll."

By the time the show ended, an exhausted Elvis embraced the Colonel, who had tears in his eyes. It seemed Elvis had spent "a lifetime waiting for the right time…the time was here at last."

He captured the hearts of all who heard him that night. Their souls surrendered to the mating call, some even tossing their most intimate undergarments on stage.

# 22

# THE IMPOSSIBLE DREAM

*This is my quest, to follow that star*

*No matter how hopeless*

~Joe Darion

Before the night ended in Vegas, the Colonel had negotiated a five-year contract for Elvis to play two months a year (February and August) in Vegas for one million dollars per year. The deal was inked on a pink tablecloth in one of the hotel cafes. For the current contract, Elvis had broken all previous records at the International Hotel, with over 100,000 tickets grossing $1.5 million.

Elvis had been through a second metamorphosis in Vegas. Keogh describes his style in the magic city as the third "distinct Elvis." She describes the period in the 50s as the time we saw the "purist Elvis." In a Lansky jacket that New Yorkers derided as fitting for a country bumpkin, Elvis was truest to himself and the image he wanted to project. When the 60s arrived and Elvis hit the big screen, he had been transformed to a "clean-cut (some would say neutered) Elvis acceptable to middle America." By the time he headlined in Vegas in the 70s, he had morphed into a glitzy, glamorous performer, all traces of the "wide-eyed country boy" banished. In this mutation, "Elvis is no longer a singer, but the greatest entertainer in the world. He is quite simply, the King of Rock and Roll."

With Vegas a mark on his jeweled karate belt, Elvis chomped at the bit. January was a long time away, and before he returned in 1970 for another month of sold-out performances, Elvis had records to cut. He was back in demand, and this time he was doing things "his way"—not in the Colonel's money-grabbing style. But his first recording session started off on a sour note. First, Elvis was sick with a cold; and for some reason, he seemed more nervous than usual. He had a hard time with "Long Black Limousine" initially, but he finally got into the song, which tells of a young girl who returns to her small hometown in a "fancy car for all the town to see." The luxurious car is a hearse and she is inside, dead. Elvis, perhaps envisioning his own mother's cortege in Memphis, comes across as almost naked, his voice gravelly from his hurting throat, revealing pure, unadulterated grief.

One of the musicians present that night, Glen Spreen, says listening to Elvis sing, feeling his soulfulness, was "almost like going to church." When he got to "In the Ghetto," his passion was so real you could almost reach out and touch it. Afraid it was too divisive, Elvis had been reticent about recording the song. He had already dipped into the political pool, where he felt an entertainer could drown if he weren't careful, with "I Can Dream," but this new song had a layer beneath the uplifting message of "I Can Dream." This song told of "poverty unanswered by an indifferent society," and it wasn't the racial overtones that Elvis resisted. It was the hopelessness of black youth, the endless cycle of poverty and crime they felt, that he wasn't sure he could convey.

Elvis need not have worried. In 1969, "In the Ghetto" sold 1.2 million copies and hit number three on the *Billboard* singles chart, while reaching number one in England. It had required 23 takes in the studio for Elvis to feel he had captured the essence of the song. In the early takes, a tender yearning reveals compassion for the underprivileged, a class to which Elvis once belonged, an economic nakedness he will never forget. It was the same sound that Marion had heard the first time Elvis sang in Sam Phillips' Sun studio. By the end, when horns and voices were overdubbed, Guralnick says Elvis projects an "almost translucent eloquence...so quietly confident in its simplicity...it makes a statement almost impossible to deny." He had tried to "right an un-rightable wrong."

Like "Suspicious Minds" and "In the Ghetto," Elvis resonated with "Only the Strong Survive." Guralnick believes these songs birthed a crossbred style, intermingling and fusing the sounds of "Old Shep" with the soul coming forth in contemporary gospel, which Elvis embraced with emotion that cried out for release. He was running "where the brave dared not go." Glen Spreen, who worked on arrangements of the new songs for Elvis, recalls he used French horns and violas "so they could blend together as a color and then be complemented by the strings." He also notes he "used syncopation with the strings — they're bowing — and I used a lot of cellos down deep and dark, especially on 'In the Ghetto,' because I wanted to bring out the darkness, the passion, as opposed to the force." He concludes he "wanted to give the vocals some realism, because I thought Elvis had a very real, very soulful voice." And he wanted to pull attention to that voice.

With the recording sessions behind him and a return trip to Vegas months away, Elvis was at loose ends. Later, Priscilla would say the only time Elvis ever felt at ease was in front of an audience. Even though he returned to Memphis, he was so restless he hopped back and forth to Los Angeles and Palm Springs continually. He did take Priscilla on another trip to Hawaii and even talked about a trip to Europe, which the Colonel nixed, arguing fans would be offended if he toured there before performing there. Elvis didn't miss the salient point — it was the Colonel who refused to book him in Europe — but he didn't confront his manager.

Bored on the home front, Elvis convinced himself Priscilla had failed as his wife because she didn't share his spiritual goals. On her end, Priscilla listened to lame excuses about why he wouldn't stay home with her and Lisa Marie. She knew Elvis was unfaithful to her, and it stung that he avoided all intimacy with her. He spent more time with Daya Mata, to whom he had turned again in his search for purpose, than he did with Priscilla.

With Daya Mata, he found a soul mate who understood the importance of seeking God's love, of wanting to give back. She saw his desire to "awaken in all these young people a closer relationship with God," and she empathized with his frustration at being unable to stay focused on the facets of his life that would accomplish that goal. Was it an impossible dream? Was his way not the right way "to march into hell for a heavenly cause"?

With no answer to his questions, Elvis continued to bounce around. He turned back to karate, which he had studied in Germany, and then shortly thereafter shifted his thoughts to Las Vegas. This time he wanted to reach forward, to touch the edge of more contemporary music. One of the songs he was particularly attracted to was "Walk a Mile in My Shoes," which took a gospel feel and turned it almost hippie. He also looked forward to singing some of his recently recorded songs before live audiences, including "In the Ghetto," "Kentucky Rain," and "Don't Cry Daddy."

Just as he knew which music he wanted to sing, Elvis knew how he wanted to look on stage. After studying pictures of Napoleon, costume designer Bill Belew decided a high-neck collar might work well for Elvis. Elvis had worn turned-up collars for years, and Belew thought that a design with a pre-formed high neckline "...would be perfect for Elvis because he is the king and it would draw attention to his face...." When he presented some sketches to Elvis, the imperial look appealed and the rest is history. Looking at his costumes over the next few years, they all sported the high-neck look. He even adopted it for casual wear.

The majestic high-necked jumpsuit for the next Vegas opening was a work of art—white wool gabardine, fitted at the waist and slit down the front. The legs, in keeping with the current fashion, were belled out at the bottom. All this was accented by exquisite embroidery embellished with real Swarovski crystals imported from Czechoslovakia. Italian gabardine from Milan added to the regal look. Dressed like a king, minutes before the show began, Elvis got the jitters. "This is when it starts getting tense," he bemoaned, anxious to get on stage but fearful of what awaited him.

In his dazzling white jumpsuit, Elvis stood in contrast to the Sweets, who were decked out in orange blouses atop black miniskirts and black go-go boots. With his trademark snarl, he let the words slip from the corner of his mouth, "Well—that's all right Mama, that's all right for you."

Despite his initial swagger, back on stage after months of anticipation, Elvis had a sudden lapse of memory, unable to remember the complete lyrics to several songs. He made light of it and made up for it the rest of the evening, wowing the audience. When he closed with his now standard encore, "Can't Help Falling in Love," he brought the house down.

As they had been after his comeback performance only months earlier, most of the reviews were positive, some even spectacular, including the one in the *Los Angeles Times* that gushed about Elvis' "flawless demonstration of vocal ability and showmanship." The *Herald-*

*Examiner* asserted, "...the new decade will belong to him." The few critical reviews smarted, as they always did, but Elvis was on a roll. For the second time, he had taken Vegas by storm. For Elvis, it was not only a second vindication of his voice; it was also affirmation he had been called to sing. "This was [his] quest, to follow that star, no matter how hopeless, no matter how far."

Underlying his outward declaration that he had hope for the future, though, Elvis' persistent self-doubt kept him worrying if it would all end.

The best cure for his worries, Elvis knew, was to stay in front of audiences. Next stop: Houston, where Elvis headlined a huge livestock and rodeo show. The first night confirmed his worst fears. The crowd, smaller than expected, seemed lost in the arena, and the poor acoustics left Elvis feeling like he was singing in a barrel. By the second show, the crowd was larger and the acoustical problems had been resolved, so Elvis perked up. The *Los Angeles Times* reported he was "masterful. His voice remained the best in rock-pop music, and his stage movements...were in perfect harmony with the music." The crowd clapped its hands and stomped its feet before rising in one accord to cheer their king.

After that night, Elvis never quite recaptured the magic in the Houston Astrodome, and although fans still knelt at his feet in adulation, he seemed oddly unattached. It was as if his arms were "too weary to reach the unreachable star." He did leave town proudly though, a sheriff's badge in hand; the beginning of what would become one of his most prized collections.

Pulling himself up, "true to [his] glorious quest," Elvis returned to the recording studio, ready to woo his fans on acetate. He cranked out several sentimental songs, including "Faded Love," "Make the World Go Away," and "Tomorrow Never Comes," and then poured his heart and soul into "Bridge Over Troubled Waters." Once again, Elvis made the songs his own, taking the best of genres as diverse as gospel and R&B, not to mention country.

Unquestionably, Elvis' genius was that he took songs written by others and often already recorded by others and gave them a fresh perspective. Norbert Putnam, the bass player for the recording session, said he was amazed Elvis would record "these very guttural, primitive songs…but I came to understand, he expressed so many things with his voice—the lyrical content had nothing to do with what was happening for him…. He was the greatest communicator of emotion that I ever knew, from beginning to end."

Whether he was in a recording studio or on the stage in Vegas, Elvis created a magnetic field. A newly appointed music director at the International Hotel wasn't enamored with Elvis before he met him, but opening night in late summer 1970 made him a believer. "I mean, I've been onstage with a lot of stars—I hate to let the air out of their balloons, but they have no idea what a star is. Jesus Christ! It was unreal. It was just a group of songs, very little production—it wasn't as organized as a lot of Vegas shows. But, boy, if you want to talk about going out and grabbing people—Elvis Presley was a happening, and what he had going will never be again. There was a vibe you could pick up in the audience—it was unbelievable. I'm not going to say to you that musically it was the best in the world. It was charisma. He just loved to put other people around his little finger and do it, and he did."

Joe Guercio, the new International Hotel music director, couldn't stop raving, describing Elvis as a free spirit who seemed oblivious to what he was doing. And Guercio wasn't the only one singing Elvis' praises. Cary Grant, who was in the audience, declared Elvis was "the greatest entertainer since Al Jolson," who had been dubbed the World's Greatest Entertainer in his day. And he was going on the road. The Colonel had booked Elvis in six cities following the Vegas engagement, and Elvis couldn't have been more elated. The Memphis *Commercial Appeal* quoted Elvis saying he was "delighted that we could work out a way to go back on the road after an absence of too many years." He even noted that he anticipated a worldwide tour in 1971. Elvis was doing what he was meant to do; in his words, "making people happy, helping them forget all their troubles for a while" as he entertained them. "I think that's what I'm on this earth to do." He would continue "to run where the brave dare not go."

In the midst of the excitement about going on the road, before Elvis finished up at the International Hotel, another source of stimulation occurred—a kidnapping plot was called in to the hotel's security office.

This was followed by a second call to the home of Joe Esposito, revealing another threat on Elvis' life. This call specifically said Elvis would be killed during the upcoming show on Saturday night. Elvis went into a tailspin, calling his friends together and telling them goodbye since he didn't know if he would ever see them again. He was counting on his friends to pull him through, and if they didn't, "I want you guys to get him. I want you to rip his goddamn eyes out. I don't want him sitting around afterward like Charlie Manson with a grin on his face, saying, 'I killed Elvis Presley.'"

That night, everyone was armed for bear, including Elvis, who packed a pistol in each boot. The hotel made sure the audience was well populated with plainclothes police, and a ready supply of oxygen and blood supplies waited backstage. Joe Moscheo, one of the Imperials, says it was nerve-racking, and everyone was glad when the night ended — that is, except Elvis. "It was crazy. It was like he was disappointed that he didn't get shot!"

The Las Vegas gig ended on a lighter note when on the last night, the band failed to come in on cue after Elvis introduced "Hound Dog." Embarrassed and exasperated, Elvis swung around to lay them low, but what he saw put him on the stage floor cracking up: a basset hound waddled, in all its fatness, through the stage curtain, making its way toward him. The laugh was on him, and he laughed 'til he cried, or as hillbillies would say, 'til the dogs came home.

The laughter energized him. He could still "dream the impossible dream."

# 23
# YOU GAVE ME A MOUNTAIN

*But this time, Lord you gave me a mountain*

*A mountain you know I may never climb*

~Marty Robbins

The impossible dream became a Ferris wheel ride over the next few years. Sometimes Elvis was on top of the world, and sometimes he stood still at the bottom, wondering who he was and what he should be doing. Even the old carny couldn't keep the Ferris wheel running smoothly all of the time. Priscilla watched with growing concern as Elvis moved farther and farther away from her. "He had bought his own image, and you couldn't have a real conversation with him; he would just discredit you and everything else." She insisted Elvis really wanted to be a family man, but "he was serving too many masters, he was too dispersed — he had all this energy, and he didn't know what to do with it."

Priscilla had Elvis nailed: "He'd go off on one thing, and then there would be an interruption; he'd go off in another direction...." That's how he ended up with a horse ranch that almost drove him back to the poor house. And that's why he once went off on a gun-buying spree, spending in excess of $20,000 in a three-day period.

Elvis' obsession with guns and badges eventually led him to the White House. He was, he once said, the hero of every comic book he had ever read, and now he wanted to be a real-life hero protecting youngsters from drugs. To do that, he would need a badge from the Bureau of Narcotics and Dangerous Drugs (BNDD). And he knew just how to get one. He would fly to Washington and talk with President Nixon.

On the flight to D.C., Elvis wrote Nixon a letter:

*"Dear Mr. President,*

*First I would like to introduce myself. I am Elvis Presley and admire you and Have Great Respect for your office. I talked to Vice President Agnew in*

*Palm Springs three weeks ago and expressed my concern for our country. The Drug Culture, the Hippie Elements, the SDS, Black Panthers, etc. do not consider me as their enemy or as they call it The Establishment. I call it America and I love it. Sir, I can and will be of any service that I can to help out."*

Elvis made it clear in his letter that he wasn't asking for a title or an appointed position, stressing he could and would do more good "if I were made a Federal agent at Large." That would enable him to help through his communications with people of all ages. However, "First and foremost I am an entertainer, but all I need is the Federal credentials."

Elvis was dead serious. He had already completed "an in-depth study of Drug Abuse and Communist Brainwashing techniques," and he was ready and willing to help in any way he could. With his letter, Elvis sent Nixon a short autobiography, including a note that he had recently been nominated as one of America's ten outstanding young men — the highest honor bestowed by the national Jaycees. And, he was the proud holder of numerous deputy badges he had received from sheriffs across the country.

Elvis dropped his letter off at the White House gates at 6:30 a.m. Later that morning, impatient for an answer, Elvis went to the Bureau of Narcotics and Dangerous Drugs. While he was there, a call came through from one of the Memphis Mafia accompanying Elvis on the trip: The President would see Elvis in 45 minutes.

The White House got more than they expected when Elvis showed up with a gun he had brought as a gift to Nixon. Secret Service personnel huddled and offered to take the gun to Nixon later. In the Oval Office, Elvis observed his surroundings in awe, then walked up to the President and introduced himself, still wearing sunglasses and holding some badges and pictures in his left hand. Nixon graciously looked at the badges and pictures Elvis laid out before him. They talked some about Elvis' desire to help young people and then Elvis went on a short rant about the Beatles, who he felt were un-American. Seemingly in agreement, Nixon responded that people at the vanguard of anti-American protests were drug users and that usually led to protests, violence, and dissent.

Bud Krogh, Nixon's staff member who had arranged the meeting for Elvis, recalls Elvis "indicated to the President in a very emotional manner that he was 'on [his] side.'" He adds that Elvis "kept repeating he wanted to be helpful, that he wanted to restore some respect for the flag, which was being lost." Elvis told the President how he had grown up poor in Tennessee but had gotten a lot from his country, and now he wanted to repay his debt. Krogh says Elvis asserted he had studied the drug culture for over ten years and could be helpful to the President in his fight against drugs.

Finally, Elvis got around to the badge he was seeking, telling the President he would be much more helpful if he was officially sanctioned by the government and that would need to be indicated by a BNDD badge. He wasn't asking for any publicity—he would be like an undercover agent.

Hesitantly, the President turned to Krogh, asking him if that was possible. "Well, sir," Krogh responded, "if you want to give him a badge, I think we can get him one." No one knows if Nixon hoped and expected Krogh to say, "No, sir, that's not possible," but he took the matter in stride, nodding and saying, "I'd like to do that. See that he gets one." For once, Elvis didn't mind smiling (remember, he thought women preferred men with sultry looks), and his grin went ear-to-ear. "Thank you very much, sir. That means a lot to me." And with that, he grabbed the President in a bear hug; something Krogh said was not, "in my limited experience, a common occurrence in the Oval Office." Nixon handled the spontaneous gesture with aplomb, patting Elvis on the back and telling him he appreciated his willingness to help.

Before he left the office, Elvis was presented with a tie clasp and cuff links engraved with the presidential seal, as well as gifts for Priscilla and Lisa. Like a kid in a candy store, Elvis couldn't get his hand out of the jar. Without thinking, he asked Nixon if he could have some of the same jewelry for the men accompanying him, adding, "You know, they've got wives, too." Krogh was left to come up with more gifts.

On good days, Elvis could still charm the socks off men and women alike. That's what he did the day he got his official BNDD badge. Even so, a few of his friends thought he was hypocritical when he showed them the badge.

Back home, Elvis' bounty still brought a positive reception.

Christmas Eve was just around the corner, and Elvis handed out some early Christmas gifts, including four Mercedes — two of the recipients were Dr. Nick and his security chief.

Christmas came and went, followed by the official awards ceremony for Elvis' Jaycees' award. His acceptance speech, which he wrote himself, spoke of his dreams. "When I was a child, ladies and gentlemen, I was a dreamer. I read comic books, and I was the hero of the comic book. I saw movies, and I was the hero in the movie. So every dream that I have ever dreamed has come true a hundred times... I'd like to say that I learned very early in life that: 'Without a song the day would never end...Without a song a man ain't got a friend...Without a song the road would never bend...Without a song....' So I keep singing a song."

The award was one of Elvis' proudest moments. He was not only recognized for his entertainment achievements but also for his philanthropy, which Elvis "consistently concealed." Listening to the citation, which spoke of his strength of character, his legendary loyalty to his friends, and his singular success in the music world, should have been the final vindication Elvis needed to make him feel secure — that his success wasn't just an illusion. But the assurance accolades brought rarely lasted longer than it took to deliver them.

Elvis' next venture was a new gospel album, where he always felt some peace. "Help Me Make It Through the Night" was beginning to seem like the theme song of his life, while "Lead Me, Guide Me" was what he really craved as he still struggled to find purpose in his life. Priscilla was beginning to wonder if her husband's purpose was to have more girlfriends than anybody in the world. It seemed that whichever state she was living in — California or Tennessee — Elvis was in the other and had a woman on his arm. His latest fling was with Joyce Boya, who had first joined the back-up band and later his bedroom troupe. Most recently, when Priscilla had returned to California to oversee decorating of a new house, Elvis invited Joyce to stay with him at Graceland. Avoiding running into one of her husband's women was becoming like a game of bumper cars for Priscilla. She was about ready to get off the ride. "I was not willing to play anymore," she acknowledged. The rules weren't fair, and the bumps hurt.

## YOU GAVE ME A MOUNTAIN

Joyce learned about the rules the hard way, too. She allegedly became pregnant with Elvis' child, but almost as if he sensed what she was about to tell him, Elvis made it clear that the "sacredness of motherhood" rendered women untouchable—they shouldn't even try "to be sexy and attracting men." Joyce held her tongue and purportedly submitted to an abortion knife a few weeks later.

If Priscilla had known, she likely would have felt lucky Elvis had married her before she had Lisa Marie. At least she hadn't gotten pregnant and then been forced to kill her baby. Maybe living a life of abstinence with Elvis wasn't the worst thing that could have happened.

Oblivious, Elvis left on his 1971 fall tour and from there back to Graceland for Christmas—his last with Priscilla. The silence between the two was deafening throughout the holidays, but no one knew what was on Priscilla's mind until Elvis announced, the night before New Year's Eve, that Priscilla had left him. He pretended not to know why, saying she had told him she no longer loved him. He seemed to hold up well initially, and going back to Vegas for his next headliner helped keep his mind off the loss of the love of his life.

He brought new songs to Vegas, including the "American Trilogy," a stirring rendition of the "Battle Hymn of the Republic," "Dixie," and "All My Trials." But it was a new ballad that revealed his soul pain. "You Gave me a Mountain" told of a young man whose wife had not only left him but had also taken his "one reason for living," his baby boy. Like the young man, Elvis's life "had been one hill after another, and [he] had climbed them all one by one." But this time, Elvis sang with a soul crying out for relief, the Lord "gave [him] a mountain, a mountain [God] knew he [might] never climb."

Elvis had bigger problems than Priscilla leaving. Joyce, who had been foolish enough to return after her assumed abortion, began to face the reality of Elvis' "messianic conviction." Summoning up courage she didn't know she had, Joyce plunged headlong into the issue she knew was killing Elvis: "Elvis, if we're gods (he had told her everyone had divinity inside them), or at least have this 'divinity' in us, why do we need drugs?"

Quietly, Elvis instructed her: "Silence is the resting place of the soul. It's sacred. And necessary for new thoughts to be born." The crux of the matter, he explained, was that the pills served a purpose: to get him as close as possible to that silence. Joyce knew Elvis was far beyond her power to help, and she slipped out the next morning before he awakened.

With Joyce gone, Priscilla came to the opening in Vegas, but then she disappeared until the last show. She came for one purpose – to tell Elvis it was over. His reaction was much worse than she expected. "He grabbed me and forcefully made love to me. It was uncomfortable and unlike any other time he'd ever made love to me before," Priscilla said sadly. And Elvis' explanation left her mystified and hurt. "This is how a real man makes love to his woman," he proclaimed. He had held Priscilla at arm's length far too long, and the amorous end to their relationship didn't make up for the lost years. Instead, it was like a slap in the face. She was "tired of the grief and the strife." She would always love him, but she couldn't take any more heartache.

The separation became official on July 26, 1972, and despite his anger and deep sense of rejection, Elvis gave Priscilla a settlement of $100,000 plus $1000 per month for alimony and $500 in child support. A little over a year later, the divorce decree was finalized. Priscilla had upped the ante, now requiring $715,000 in cash in addition to $6000 per month for ten years, not including $4200 per month in spousal support for a year, $4000 per month in child support and a 5 percent cut of Elvis' new publishing company. With her half of the house in Hillcrest, Priscilla's total take approached two million dollars.

Elvis could have cared less about the money; it was the public humiliation that almost destroyed him. Some say Elvis never again found even a semblance of peace. Priscilla was ready to look to the future, but Elvis seemed chained to the past. She was on the top of the mountain looking down at Elvis, who wondered if he would ever be able to make the climb.

# 24
# SEPARATE WAYS

*All that's left between us are the memories we shared*

*Of times we thought we cared for each other*

~Richard Mainegra and Bobby West

Elvis floundered about, unable to get his arms around why Priscilla left. She knew how he was long before she married him. All those other women meant nothing to him—except when he was with them. He always came back to Priscilla, so why would she leave him? As he played the recording "Where Does Love Go?" over and over, the question rolled in his mind like a wheel on a rutted road.

He didn't feel like going back to work, but a recording session had already been scheduled in Los Angeles. The first song he cut pushed him deeper into melancholy. "Separate Ways" told the story of a little boy (changed to a girl for Elvis' rendition) who didn't understand why his mom and dad were not together. As Elvis almost whispered the line, "The tears that she will cry when I have to say goodbye will tear at my heart forever," his heartache was palpable in the stillness of the recording room. His yearning yielded his voice hopeless.

And so went the rest of the recording session. It was as if every song had been selected by Elvis to punish himself, or at least to accentuate his despondency. "For the Good Times" stirred up memories that were still too tender to rest easy in his mind. Elvis wasn't ready to "say a word about tomorrow." Fittingly, the night's session ended with "Where Do I Go from Here?" Elvis felt like the fool in the song—there was no one left to listen. If he knew the way, he'd go back home, but too many bridges had been crossed and burned. He knew something was missing in his life—and it wasn't just Priscilla—but he didn't know where to go to find it.

For the first time in his life, Elvis was singing for himself, not his audience. Bob Abel, one of the filmmakers he worked with on an upcoming documentary, captured the essence of Elvis at that time in his life: "...I think there was a part of him that felt hollow, that he was a nobody; there were parts of him that he could not explore." Abel acknowledged Elvis "...had incredible native intelligence, the ability to read a human being, to watch someone's eyes and look inside their soul," but at the same time Elvis was hard to read. What Abel found was that the way inside Elvis' mind and soul was through his gospel music. As he watched Elvis unwind after rehearsals, often with the Stamps, it was like watching a flawless diamond come forth from a lump of coal.

On the road, Elvis could catch the excitement of a crowd and respond to it like a preacher stirred by "amens" in his congregation. Abel, and his partner Pierre Adidge, set out to capture this almost indefinable connection. It was like trying to film a spirit leaving the body at death and soar through the air. To find the source of spirit on the stage, Abel and Adidge went back to the beginning with Elvis, asking him to tell how he started singing on stage.

His mind gliding back in time, Elvis reached back further than his inaugural stage appearance. He recalled, "I first realized that I could sing at about two years of age." Almost shyly, he told the filmmakers only people in his neighborhood and at his church knew he could sing—he said he kept his voice a secret in school until the 11th grade when his teacher recommended him for a talent show at Overton Park in Memphis: "The first time it happened, the first time that I appeared onstage it scared me to death, man. I didn't know what I'd done." His classmates couldn't believe the oddly dressed, shy boy could sing—and sing with a passion that captivated everyone listening. Elvis said he still doesn't know what happened on stage that day, but he knew it was an enchanted moment—one he re-created every time he stepped before a crowd. "I work absolutely to the audience, whether it's six or six thousand, it doesn't really matter; they bring it out of me—the inspiration, the ham." Perhaps for the first time, Elvis admitted some of his shenanigans were an act, despite his protestations over the years that his gyrating leg was a natural, uncontrollable movement.

In one of the few times Elvis confided how much he hated what the Colonel had made him do, he told the makers of the documentary that some of his films made him "violently ill." He never directly attacked the

Colonel, but he made it clear he personally was left out of the decision-making process about what was good for him. "I don't think anyone was consciously trying to harm me. It was just Hollywood's image of me was wrong, and I knew it, and I couldn't say anything about it, couldn't do anything about it." Elvis explained he kept hoping they would "give me a chance to show some kind of acting ability or do a very interesting story, but it did not change, it did not change, and so I became very discouraged." He concluded with, "They couldn't have paid me no amount of money in the world to make me feel self-satisfaction inside."

The boy who had chosen his way had allowed others, especially the Colonel, to shape his career in the same fashion he had tried to make Priscilla into his ideal woman. "Any Way You Want Me To Be" seemed to have been the theme song of his movie career, and one wonders why Elvis didn't exert enough energy to do it "his way" instead of the Colonel's way. Sadly, both he and Priscilla learned there was no pride in trying to be what someone else wants you to be rather than being true to yourself.

With Elvis, it was more complicated than that. Marion Keisker, who really should be credited with discovering Elvis at the Memphis Recording Studio, perceived the essence of Elvis in the weeks and months he kept coming by her office: "He was like a mirror. Whatever you were looking for, you were going to find in him. It was not in him to lie or say anything malicious. He had all the intricacy of the very simple."

Perhaps it was that simplicity, that innocence, which not only compelled him to be molded by others at times but also touched audiences with such mystery. Even in the midst of sporadic health problems, the enchantment held. His four performances in June 1972 at Madison Square Garden sold out (this was significant since Elvis had never sung in New York City in the more than 15 years he had been performing), and flattering media coverage was profuse, with the *New York Times* calling him "a prince from another planet." In a story that helped wipe out the embarrassment of singing to a hound dog on the *Steve Allen Show*, Chris Chase compared Elvis to other "special champions" that come along "once in a great while, people like Joe Louis, Jose Capablanca, Joe DiMaggio, someone in whose hands the way a thing is done becomes more important than the thing itself." Chase closed by saying Elvis' grace made the act look as easy and inevitable as DiMaggio's hitting a baseball. Elvis "stood there at the end, his arms stretched out, the great gold cloak giving him wings, a champion, the only one in his class."

It was a far cry from the days when preachers condemned him from the pulpit, when mayors issued restraining orders on his legs. Finally, it seems, his image had turned from dark to golden. Elvis never forgot, though, that "the image is one thing and the human being another." When he answered a reporter's question with, "It's very hard to live up to an image," Elvis revealed some of the pressure he constantly felt as a public figure.

Back in Memphis after the filming of his documentary and his New York concerts, Elvis was at loose ends. Priscilla was gone, and he knew "there was nothing left to do but go [their] separate ways and pick up the pieces left behind them."

Linda Thompson pulled Elvis from his doldrums, at least temporarily. The reigning Miss Tennessee, Linda wasn't simply beautiful, she met his needs, watching over him. She wasn't as malleable as Priscilla, but she cared, and he needed that right now. Looking back, Linda says, "...my life just revolved around him. We kind of just geared off each other and understood the moods and became what the other needed for the moment." Elvis needed someone to surround him with unconditional love like a young puppy needs the warmth of its mother. And Linda gave him the security he craved. Some called Linda a "lifer," unlike the in-and-out girls the Memphis Mafia christened "queen for a day."

Linda helped Elvis regain his equilibrium. For a change, he had something to look forward to when he woke up at 4 p.m. each day; a reason to lose weight, to regain his old excitement and charm. Selecting the songs for the NBC concert became an obsession—they had to be his best ever. He picked through old ones he had used in concerts but never recorded, including "What Now My Love" and "The Twelfth of Never." And, of course, he wanted to include "My Way" and "You Gave Me a Mountain," songs that came straight from the heart of his life.

Though the audience for the taped television show rocked with the same frenzy that always accompanied a live performance, Elvis seemed somewhat detached. Guralnick notes he didn't seem caught up in the hysteria that usually drove his "manic energy." Only at the end did he get into the music, getting turned on by "An American Trilogy." As he came back from the "glory, glory, hallelujah" that had taken him "far, far away," Guralnick says Elvis jumped into "A Big Hunk O' Love" before ending with "Can't Help Falling in Love," where he "ends down on one knee, his back to the audience, his cape spread out in that familiar pose of humble adoration, combined with self-adoration, that the world has come to accept as Elvis in any language."

Some say the money raised for the charity benefit eclipsed Elvis's lackluster performance. Joe Guercio sensed something different about Elvis that night, "…there was just not as much wind blowing through the show…you could just feel it."

Were the ongoing health problems pulling him down? Or was Elvis still mourning Priscilla, even with Linda shoring him up? He had yearned that "maybe someday, somewhere along the way, another love [would find him]," and it seemingly had. Why was it not enough? Why was it harder and harder for him to find the magic connection—in his love life and on the stage?

# 25

# BRIDGE OVER TROUBLED WATERS

*When you're down and out...when times get rough*

*I will lay me down*

~Paul Simon

After the excitement of the satellite benefit wound down, Elvis had a hard time getting himself up for his scheduled Vegas appearance. He didn't feel well, and a string of doctors couldn't pinpoint why. At one point the diagnosis was flu; later it was pneumonia; he was so congested, several shows had to be cancelled. Even after his symptoms disappeared, Elvis couldn't shake his despondency. Those closest to him talked among themselves, wondering if he was taking too much medication for his depression, but they were afraid to confront him. They all agreed Priscilla was at the root of Elvis' problems, but that was a taboo subject, too.

On February 18, 1973, everyone's worst fears were realized — several men attempted to attack Elvis onstage. The Memphis Mafia burst into action and Elvis himself used his karate skills to take care of one assailant. When the scary situation calmed down, Elvis's first thought was that someone had discovered he was an undercover agent with the federal government, and the drug cartel had sent some goons to take him out. The more he thought, though, the more he believed it was Mike Stone, Priscilla's new boyfriend, who had instigated the attack. He wanted Elvis totally out of the picture so he could not only become Priscilla's husband but also Lisa Marie's father, Elvis reasoned irrationally. At one point, he asked Red to hire a contract killer to take care of Mike before he came to his senses and decided to forget the whole thing.

The quick anger, the convoluted thinking, and the urge to do something violent could have been the result of medication, but it could also have been the culmination of his rising humiliation and anger that

BRIDGE OVER TROUBLED WATERS

Priscilla had left him. He couldn't deal with it, couldn't understand how she could leave him. He began acting weirdly on stage, sometimes inexplicably attacking his musicians in front of audiences. Bobby Wood, keyboard player, said Elvis had become a totally different person. Sometimes he arrived more than an hour late, and one night he failed to show up at all. Drummer Jerry Carrigan said Elvis "...seemed like he was miserable...He just didn't seem to care." Reviews were awful, with the *Hollywood Reporter* describing his voice as "thin, uncertain, and strained." The critic's description of Elvis' physical appearance was devastating: "He's not just a little out of shape, not just a little chubbier than usual, the Living Legend is fat...." But adoring fans didn't seem to notice. They loved him—his voice was like heaven, and no two-bit reporter was going to change that. Whether it was the critical review or his undying commitment to his fans, Elvis finally pulled himself out of his doldrums and ended the Vegas series on a high note, receiving a standing ovation for his rendition of "What Now My Love." To Elvis, that was proof everyone was worrying needlessly.

While Elvis' emotions rose and descended like a boat in tumultuous high seas, the Colonel was wheeling and dealing. He worked out an agreement with RCA in which they paid $5.4 million for total rights to all of Elvis' past records. As per the renegotiated contract between Parker and Elvis, the old carny pocketed $2.6 million. And the Colonel inked another RCA contract for seven years, each of which had a guarantee of $500,000 for four new singles and two new albums per year. The Colonel's take on this contract, $1.75 million. Elvis didn't blink an eye, although Vernon and others knew the Colonel was robbing Elvis in a desperate move to cover his mounting debts from too much time in casinos. Later, Jack Soden, president of Elvis Presley Enterprises, described the lucrative deal the Colonel conned Elvis into signing (giving him half of Elvis' earnings) as "a stunningly bad business move—right up there with the Indians selling Manhattan for twenty-four dollars."

On the next road tour, begun in April 1973, this time for nine days on the West Coast, Elvis' downward slide quickened. By the time he arrived in Tahoe in May for a 17-day booking, he was near the bottom, cancelling the final four days of the tour. The Colonel swung into action, determined to find the source of the multiple prescriptions that were affecting Elvis' ability to perform. A master manipulator, the Colonel tried conniving the doctors into slowing down the flow of pills. When that didn't work, he resorted to threatening them.

A few weeks later, matters came to a head when Elvis' behavior on stage became so bizarre it bordered on the obscene, He modified the lyrics of "Love Me Tender" to the point they could have been classified X-rated. When he made disparaging remarks about the owner of the Hilton, the Colonel had had enough and jumped Elvis. Already overwrought, Elvis lost it. Before the argument ended, Elvis had fired the Colonel or the Colonel had quit, according to which man was telling the story. Elvis and Vernon vacillated between being glad to be rid of the money-hungry, wheeling-dealing old man and being scared to death they couldn't manage without him. Finally, Elvis caved and called the Colonel, and by most reports, Elvis apologized. What mattered most to Elvis was his music, and if he had to put up with the Colonel to keep reaching audiences, then by blimey, he could do it.

Parker's iron-fisted management of Elvis, while lucrative, cost Elvis many of his dreams. He directed him away from dramatic movies and finally nixed Elvis' last opportunity at a serious acting role. After a stage show in the mid-70s, Barbara Streisand approached Elvis about co-starring with her in a remake of *A Star is Born*. It would have been a perfect vehicle for Elvis—both for his image and for his career quest—but the Colonel wasn't pleased with the offer of money, calling it a "cheap deal," and managed to kill the prospect of a "real" movie.

Elvis felt caught in a vortex. He despised the Colonel but lacked the confidence to shed his nemesis. He loved Priscilla, but because he could not give up other women, he could not hold her.

Sinking, he went to see Sri Daya Mata, and she recalls Elvis' struggle. "I think that things were not turning out the way he hoped they would. He didn't have the energy, the enthusiasm, the feeling that he had in his earlier years. He was not at peace." Elvis seemed to have lost hope.

Anyone who knew Elvis well realized he couldn't handle rejection. Insecure from his early years, he never totally shed the feeling he wasn't worthy of all that had been given him. When Priscilla left, it was like

God was punishing him because he wasn't good enough. The old fears crept back, and worse than that, the *whole world* knew he had been cast aside. Public humiliation might not have trumped his inner shame, but it contributed to his overall malaise.

When Priscilla met Elvis at the Los Angeles County Superior Courthouse in Santa Monica on October 9, she was shocked at how he looked — not just his physical appearance, but also the sense that he was a diminished person, that he had an emptiness about him she had never seen before.

Within days after the divorce papers were signed, Elvis' breathing became so erratic he chartered a plane to get him back to Memphis, where he was admitted to Baptist Memorial Hospital. The doctors were stymied about what was causing Elvis to have so many health problems. They could find no reason for his shortness of breath and his swollen appearance, and they were concerned about the needle marks on his arms. Finally, Elvis admitted an acupuncturist had been using syringes instead of needles — and when Dr. Nick called the so-called doctor for an explanation, he found he had been injecting Elvis with liquid Demerol almost daily. Dr. Nick weaned Elvis off the drugs, and he was also treated for an enlarged intestine, as well as a liver problem. For the first time in years, Elvis began to feel like himself again. He appeared scared enough to finally take back the control of his life that he had turned over to massive amounts of medication.

Unfortunately, Elvis' fear — and thus his progress — didn't last long. Dr. Nick tried to control Elvis' doses, at one point even providing daily packets that he or his assistant personally delivered so Elvis would not have access to more medication than prescribed for one day. Linda was a big help during this time, alerting Dr. Nick if packages arrived from doctors in California or Nevada. And, she tried to keep Elvis' spirits up and his irritation down, especially when he was upset with Dr. Nick for holding back his pills. The good doctor remembers, "Linda was a really good influence on him. She tried to help him any way she could. She would bring out a different side of Elvis, his humor, his 'carrying on.'"

In spite of his health problems, Elvis recorded another album, but everyone in the studio sensed he wasn't himself. Amazingly, by the time he made it to his next Vegas engagement, he was seemingly in improved health and in better humor, although his temperament was still dicey, partly because of all the infighting among his closest associates. Linda was doing her part to keep him in good humor, voluntarily disappearing when he brought a new girl around.

Back in Memphis, Elvis performed to sell-out crowds in his first live performances in his hometown in 13 years. Two months later, he was on the road for a California tour and then on to Tahoe, where one newspaper reported he was "listless, uninspired, and downright tired." Some reports cited flu as the problem. Whatever the cause, Elvis was getting worse, and no one knew how to stop the descent that was smothering his spirit.

For a while, Elvis turned back to karate, hoping it would help him heal. Vernon wasn't around much during this period, having his own disenchantment—Dee had decided she wanted no more of the Presley life. Elvis was glad to see her gone. No love lost there.

Elvis kept pushing, going back to Vegas following a 21-day tour where he and the Colonel split a $1.5M profit. Fans continued to overlook or just be amused by his stage antics, but more and more, the critics were wiping up the floor with him. In Vegas, Elvis turned to ballads and blues, temporarily abandoning other genre, perhaps because slow songs that spoke of lost love flowed easily from his soul-sickness. Where he had once delivered syrupy love songs with finesse—his voice clearly feeling the emotion of his heart, now his voice virtually shook instead of delivering the notes with a smooth vibrato. Almost overnight, the crowds began to lose their rock-solid connection with the star. It's hard to know if Elvis discerned he no longer pulled an audience like a magnet. His success had been built on his instinctive ability to read an audience and respond with what they loved, but now he couldn't bridge the gap between his heart and theirs.

Nothing seemed to satisfy Elvis, even Linda. When he needed a friend, "[she was] sailing right behind him." But sometimes he turned from her. He was back to having a parade of girls in and out of his room whenever he could think up some place to send Linda for a few days. That helped as long as one of the girls was with him, but when he was alone, he reverted to medicine to subdue his dark emotions. The only experience that seemed to give him pleasure was presenting people with overgenerous gifts, and that lasted about as long as the "thank you" he received. Unable to escape his tortured mind, where he was often preoccupied with a multitude of issues (disenchantment with his career, inability to maintain a long-term relationship with women he loved, boredom, spiritual emptiness, etc.), he even turned to cocaine for a short time. Once again, he landed in a hospital, this time for two weeks. While he was there, Vernon had a heart attack and joined him in the hospital, occupying a room next to his son.

Elvis disengaged from Linda about this time, temporarily replacing her with Sheila Ryan. It didn't take Sheila long to realize that she progressed from being girlfriend to mother: "You were expected to take care of him, and basically that's what the role was…to get him things in the middle of the night. He needed water, he needed pills, he needed Jell-O, he needed to be read to. That was what I did." She adds that part of the relationship was still romantic—Elvis would sing tender love songs to her on the balcony, and he constantly gave her generous gifts. But that only embarrassed her, making her feel like a "kept woman" instead of a true love.

In performances, Elvis started delivering long monologues, sometimes before he sang, sometimes in the middle of a song. One time, with Sheila sitting in a booth alongside Priscilla, who had brought Lisa Marie to see her father perform, Elvis went on a tangent after he pounded out, "You Gave Me A Mountain."

"I want to make one thing clear. I've been singing that song for a long time, and a lot of people kind of got it associated with me because they think it's of a personal nature. It is not…it has nothing to do with me personally or my ex-wife, Priscilla. She's right here. Honey stand up. Come out, honey. Come out, come on out. Turn around, let them see you. Boy she's—she's a beautiful chick. I'll tell you for sure, boy. Boy, I knows 'em when I picks 'em. You know? Goddamn."

Then Elvis introduced Lisa Marie, followed by Sheila, whom he instructed to stand up and turn around, "turn completely around," demanding that she hold up her right hand to show off her ring. With another expletive, he let the audience know it was a big thrill for him to have a ring on Sheila's finger.

Turning back to Priscilla, Elvis tried to convince the audience he and Priscilla were the best of friends, that the divorce was caused by his traveling so much and not by another man or woman. He let the audience know he had given Priscilla a $2 million settlement, and after that, he even bought her a mink coat. In turn, he bragged, Priscilla bought him a $42,000 white Rolls-Royce. From there he talked about his Stutz and managed a play on words by saying Mike Stone was not a "stud."

On and on he went, rambling and mumbling until he finally wound down with the story surrounding "Softly As I Leave You." But it wasn't over. A few songs later, he took off on another monologue, this time about the woman who accused him of getting her pregnant. When he abandoned that train of thought, he moved to an explanation of how ill he had been. "In this day and time you can't even get sick. You are *strung out.* By God, I'll tell you something, friend, I have never been strung out in my life, except on music." In a tone that ranged from dramatic to sorrowful, Elvis complained about being accused of being strung out on heroin when he really had the flu, running a fever of 102 degrees. By the time he finished his rant about what he would do if anybody ever made such accusations again, the crowd was cheering him.

Priscilla's reaction was in dramatic contrast to the fans' response: "I was in shock." She stressed Elvis would never have shared such raw emotions with an audience in the past. "You know, singing was always his way of venting his emotions. how he felt about something—and he'd get onstage and sing his heart out....This was out of character, for someone who had so much pride, you know—everything that he was against, he was displaying. It was like watching a different person." He needed a bridge over troubled waters to ease his mind, but his "silver girl" had "sailed on," and he couldn't find his way.

# 26
# EDGE OF REALITY

*Here's where life's dream lies disillusioned*

~Bernie Baum, Bill Giant, Florence Key

It wasn't only what he was doing on stage that was of concern; off stage Elvis went on a buying spree that lasted almost two weeks. More than a dozen friends benefitted from his largess, driving home brand-new vehicles. He even bought his latest maid a car, followed by a car for his cook's brother and a house for the cook himself. Billy Smith and his family became the proud new owners of a doublewide trailer to be placed on the ground of Graceland, and Charlie Hodge got the keys to a new boat. It was like he couldn't stop spending, and one wonders if he felt so alone he was trying to lock in what little friendship and loyalty he had among those closest to him. He was "on the borderline of doom."

Back on stage, Elvis tried to keep up appearances, but it was clear to everyone around him he couldn't go on much longer. A myriad of tests revealed he had an ulcer, and the prescribed treatment seemed to perk him up. When Jerry Schilling came to visit him in the hospital and announced he was going to marry Myrna Smith of the Sweet Inspirations, Elvis immediately offered to buy them a house. His explanation: "...your mother died when you were a year old, and you never had a home, and I wanted to be the one to give it to you." Kind and generous, it was like the old Elvis had been reborn. The only problem was that he was running out of money, and both Vernon and the Colonel feared the golden well was about to dry up as onstage dialogues continued to dominate performances. Press reviews were brutal, with one declaring Elvis was "paunchy, depressed, and living in fear."

Watching him disintegrate in front of her eyes, Sheila saw him as "the boy in the bubble." His life was so insular he had lost touch with himself and the world. He vacillated from thinking he was nobody—a kid who had had a little success—to somebody, a "living legend." The bottom line was he didn't know who he was any more. On his 40th birthday, he sat alone at Graceland in what the Memphis *Commercial Appeal* described as "self-imposed seclusion."

Linda tried to fend off the growing number of stories about Elvis' drug problems, telling *People* magazine the rumors were absurd, "Why, Elvis is a federal narcotics officer!" In the privacy of Graceland, though, she gently confronted Elvis, who conceded, "I'm self-destructive." He added there wasn't a lot he could do about it, and the conversation ended. Dark shadows followed him, and he couldn't shake them.

After continuing treatment for his stomach problems, Elvis was ready for another Vegas engagement, to be followed by a two-week tour. Thinking he was back on his feet, Elvis made a down payment of $75,000 on a Boeing 707 jet. Before the jet arrived, he had a bad episode where he struggled to breathe and was admitted once again to the hospital. Almost overnight, he lost 10 pounds, perhaps a result of a recent diagnosis of twisted intestines. If it hadn't been determined that this was a congenital defect, one would have wondered if his insides had kinks because his emotional life was tied up in knots. Where he had once found release for his intense feelings in music, he now found himself unable to get inside the lyrics, to find his core at the depth of the songs. He suffered with fears he couldn't put into words. Physical and emotional pangs beat incessantly on his insides, begging for relief.

When everyone else thought he couldn't go on any longer, Elvis surprised them, pulling himself up enough for Vegas that he received a standing ovation from his fans, although the media continued to point out his shortcomings. Perhaps their description of him as "pale and overweight" woke him up, at least temporarily, because he lost some weight and his performances on the road tour seemed to motivate him more than they had in recent years. From rock songs to "How Great Thou Art," the old Elvis seemed to be coming back. To assist in the transformation, he had cosmetic surgery to make the area around his eyes look younger. Interestingly, Billy thought the surgery did more harm than good. "He always had those sleepy, sexy eyes. And they took the droop out. The droop was part of his mystique."

Elvis struggled to stay excited about his performances, but he didn't have to do anything to ramp up his excitement about his new jet (the deal for the first one had fallen through), which was going to be called the "Lisa Marie." The jet would have an executive-style bathroom (complete with a gold sink and gold faucets) beside his private, lavishly appointed bedroom. In keeping with his love of television and music, the plane would have four televisions and a 52-speaker setup. A conference room outfitted in teak was created to the side of the large, luxurious seats in the main body of the plane.

On the stage, a rampage of emotions revealed itself. Guralnick noted that Elvis' rendition of "How Great Thou Art" in his next concert had transmuted into a painful cry, which some felt crossed the bounds of appropriateness. Only Pentecostal churches accepted the rawness of emotion pouring from Elvis' soul. Similarly, his delivery of "I'll Never Walk Alone" lost the hope engendered by the words of the song, replaced by a distressing dilemma—he believed but questioned his beliefs.

Sick in body and soul, Elvis struggled to keep his audience engaged, twice throwing his guitar into the crowd, saying he no longer needed it and once giving away a $6,500 ring in the hope of getting his audience excited. It was, Guralnick avows, as if his head were filled with odd voices, an echo of the critics who long ago had mocked and derided his singing.

Over the next two days, Elvis distributed expensive jewelry, racking up a bill for $85,000. Again caught up in a gift-giving mood, he bought a small jet for the Colonel, who promptly turned it down. Others jumped at the chance to get a gift, including the 14 who received Cadillacs one Sunday afternoon. A lady, whom Elvis had never met, had been in the showroom looking at cars, and Elvis generously added the one she liked to the purchases for his friends. Later, he bought a Mark IV for one of his doctors and another for Jerry Kennedy. Linda got a Seville, as did Elvis' friend Ron Pietrafeso. Joe Esposito's girlfriend got an Eldorado.

Elvis had always been generous with his money, but this was different. It was like he couldn't stop spending, as if he was either trying to buy friendship or pay down a debt for something he had done wrong. Or, maybe it simply made him feel better about himself—that he really was "somebody" because he could help others. And, to make up to Lisa Marie that he was not a fulltime father, he showered her with gifts.

# MY WAY

Sheila disappeared about this time, having had enough of sharing Elvis with whichever woman he happened to fancy at the moment. Elvis picked up a 19-year-old, Melissa Blackwood, as a temporary replacement. She was shocked at how he revealed himself to her before they had had time to get to know one another. Before their first night was over, he had given her a car and then asked her to move in to Graceland. Sensing she was about to get in over her head, Melissa refused, and he let her go, allowing her to keep the car.

Next he met a hostess who worked with the Memphis Grizzlies. Jo Cathy Brownlee received a Grand Prix the first night, just as Melissa had. He tried to persuade her to go to Vegas with him, but she declined. Sadly, Elvis didn't make it to Vegas without an emergency landing in Dallas when he couldn't get his breath. Later, when he finished the trip, his opening night reflected his poor health, and *Variety* not only described him as overweight but also having a "lack of stamina and poor vocal projection." Linda, who had come out for the opening, said Elvis was "out of it," even if his audience did not realize it. "He was just barely going through the motions; he was lethargic and uncoordinated." She adds she thought Elvis realized "he was in trouble."

Although Elvis made it through two shows, the rest of the engagement had to be cancelled "due to illness." Vegas, no longer a challenge — he had conquered the city long ago —, didn't have the power to pull him out of himself. The city where he first failed to reach an audience, the town in the desert where he could hide out with other celebrities, and the place where he had returned in triumph no longer mattered to him. In fact, at one of his last concerts in Vegas, he told the crowd, "I hate Las Vegas."

The Colonel fretted — not just for Elvis but also for himself. His had amassed millions of dollars in gambling debts, and now he wasn't sure the show would go on long enough to pay them off. In addition to stomach issues, Elvis was now diagnosed with early chronic obstructive pulmonary disease. At the hospital, Elvis was cared for by a matronly nurse (upon whom he bestowed a Pontiac Grand Prix). She gave him such good care he asked her to work for him fulltime when he was dismissed to go home. Under her watchful eye, he began to improve. As with Linda, Elvis "evoked a protective" quality in the nurse, Marion

Cocke.

Seeing Elvis was in good hands, Linda headed back to California where she was working on her own career. Although she always came running when Elvis was sick and needed her, being around him was becoming harder and harder. "I felt a strong sense of security on one level—and then real anxiety on another. I mean, he was who he was; he wasn't going to change...there was also this very naïve, this almost infantile quality about him—very innocent and very pure, kind of pitiful." But she wasn't his mother, even if he sometimes called her "Mommy," and she knew she needed to escape. And Elvis momentarily thought, "If she's not real, then I'm condemned to the edge of reality."

His health deteriorating, Elvis went through the motions of performing on whatever tour or engagement the Colonel set up for him. He had no choice; he had given away most of his money or spent it on his growing gun collection or other expensive "toys." On stage he sometimes had memory lapses with old songs, and some said he appeared half-asleep throughout performances. He rallied himself for "My Way" in Long Beach, where a local newspaper related, "An eerie silence filled the concert hall when he sang, 'And now the end is near'... It was like witnessing a chilling prophecy."

But for other songs, Elvis knew he had lost his passion and excitement. He also perceived, in his words, "These people, they don't care if I'm good or bad. I can do anything, and they still love it." Elvis felt more alone than he ever had before; it seemed all of his old friends were disappearing, one by one, to go on with their lives, perhaps realizing the end was in sight. Signs were mounting; at one point the orchestra director, Joe Guercio, bemoaned, "You know, all he can do now is die." Another forewarning, and as if he heard it, Elvis tried to pull himself together, returning for help from Dr. Elias Ghanem, a Palestinian refugee from whom he had sought assistance in the past, as had many other stars.

After following Dr. Ghanem's medical advice, which was again not effective, Elvis went on his fifth tour of the year. Fans continued their devotion to the star, but the *Newport Times-Herald* surmised the reverence, the idolization, was more "for what he was, what he symbolizes, rather than for what he is or how he sings now." The reporter added Elvis' music no longer had soul, that there was "no driving power behind his voice." And Elvis recognized it was true. Everyone else knew it, too, and that cut deeply. One writer noted Elvis had been breaking hearts for more than 20 years, "and Saturday afternoon in the Summit—in a completely new and unexpected way—he broke mine."

Seeing the legend acting more like a drunk on a street corner than a king, "least of all [the king] of rock 'n' roll," was like watching a falling meteor, waiting for it to strike the earth and explode. The writer, Bob Claypool of the *Houston Post*, said the audience didn't seem to notice, but "...for some of us, it would never be the same, because the man who had given us the original myth of rock 'n' roll—the man who created it and *lived* it—was now, for whatever reason, taking it all back."

"Reality, reality, reality, reality."

*Author's Note: Today, it is widely accepted that some people are pre-wired to be addictive and thus the first drug or drink they take leads to a disease over which they have no control. Elvis was hooked from the first pill he took from his sergeant. He should not be judged too harshly – in his day no one knew that for some people, one pill is too much, and a thousand is never enough. Elvis received only minimal treatment for addiction, likely from doctors who had little or no knowledge about the disease, and it was not enough.*

# 27

# CRYING IN THE CHAPEL

*I've searched and I've searched*
*But I couldn't find the way on earth*
*To gain peace of mind.*

~Artie Glenn

Rumors had hit the street that Red and Sonny, along with another former bodyguard employee, were working on a "tell all" book about their time with Elvis. Payback was going to be hell, Elvis realized, as his former friends—people who had benefitted from working with him for years—decided to take out their anger and frustration on him because he had let them go. In desperation, he called Red, trying to assure him all was well and he would always try to take care of him. When Red tried to explain how hurt he had been, Elvis responded, "All of us were hurt..." and then quoted both "Desiderata" ("Listen to the dull and ignorant, because they, too, have a story to tell") and Hank Williams' "You never walked in that man's shoes and saw things through his eyes." Seeing he was getting nowhere, Elvis ended with, "Worried about the book? I don't think so, not on my part. You do whatever you have to do. I just want you and Pat to know I'm still here."

Protestations aside, Elvis was worried. And he stewed more when he read in the *Star* about his conversation with Red, which the paper described as a "dramatic plea to his ex-bodyguard: 'Don't write that book about me.'"

John Lennon offered a shrewd take on Elvis' entourage, especially the Memphis Mafia, including Sonny and Red: "The King is always killed by his courtiers. He is overfed, overindulged, and overdrunk to keep him tied to his throne. Most people in the position never wake up." And, he could have added, they rarely realize they are being manhandled or manipulated or used for ulterior, often personal motives. Fortunately, the betrayers were few, but the damage done by Sonny and

Red later took a life of its own.

In the meantime, Elvis continued to search for new people with whom to surround himself.

About this time he met a girl, Ginger Lee, who seemed to be a keeper, and almost overnight she replaced Linda in his heart. In some ways Linda was relieved, knowing in her inner being she couldn't save Elvis. "He was going to go ahead and kill himself, no matter what I did. I couldn't make him happy, and I knew he wasn't going to change." So she left, sad but thankful not to feel responsible for Elvis any longer.

Elvis began to feel better, but he continued to take heavy doses of medication for his multiple ailing organs. At one point, he thought he had overdosed, telling Geller (who had returned to the fold), "This is it— I'm going out. I—ah—took too much—or someone gave me the wrong thing. I'm going...I'm leaving my body. I'm dying." Geller describes Elvis' eyes as "strange, haunted," adding, "he stared at me, taking in deep gulps of air and breathing erratically." In addition to medical help, Elvis sought out Rex Humbard, the television evangelist, asking him if he should give up singing and devote himself to God. Humbard assured him he was serving God through his singing, and then they knelt and prayed, with Elvis weeping quietly, feeling God's presence despite the turmoil in his soul.

After a momentary sense of peace, Elvis soon returned to his malaise. The Memphis *Press-Scimitar* summed up the feeling of many: "...one walks away wondering how much longer it can be before the end comes, perhaps suddenly, and why the king of Rock 'n' Roll would subject himself to potential ridicule by going onstage so ill-prepared. Why carry on? For fame? He's perhaps the best-known, best-loved performer of all time...." The writer, Bill Burk, ended by saying that despite Elvis' decline, "They [fans] keep coming back....Once a king, always a king. Maybe that's it. And just maybe they're still coming because they think it might be the last time around."

Elvis may have wondered too, because he made out his will, although he had resisted doing so for years. His father was to be the executor and trustee, and provisions were made for Lisa Marie, Vernon, and his grandmother, with Vernon responsible for taking care of any other relatives who might need emergency assistance, with the caveat that such help should not deprive his three primary beneficiaries of their needs. Eventually, everything would go into a trust for Lisa-Marie. He had given his friends—and most of his relatives—plenty during his lifetime, having once said to Larry Geller, "…what profiteth it to gain the world if you couldn't share your good fortune with your friends." And he had done just that. After his death, his primary concern would be for his daughter.

Elvis' last few tours continued in the same vein as those in recent years—lackluster and erratic. After constant bickering with Ginger, she temporarily abandoned him, and he turned back to Kathy, telling her in broken words about his pain and his fears, repeatedly asking, "'How will they remember me?'" Then, tearfully, he bemoaned, "'They're not going to remember me. I've never done anything lasting. I've never done a class film.'" In a quick mood swing, Elvis asserted he had been born to sing, "'…to make people happy with music. And I'll never stop until the day I die.'"

After ignoring the changes in their king for eons, fans finally began to fade—standing ovations became an act of the past. Desperate for love, Elvis handed out a few more cars, including Lincoln Mark V's to Geller and Kathy. But everyone around him had a growing feeling, according to Guralnick, that "they had set out on a doomed voyage, captainless, rudderless, with no hope of turning back." Those closest to him knew Elvis was crying out for help, but they knew offering it would bring swift annihilation.

On the road, Elvis occasionally rallied, his voice stronger. He lost some weight, and his bloated appearance, caused by his stomach problems and cortisone treatments, improved. He fooled everyone—including himself—into believing he was better. In his final concert, his 56th of the year, Elvis performed before a full house in Indianapolis, Indiana. Just before the show, RCA made a special presentation: a plaque commemorating his two millionth record pressed by the recording company. Pumped, Elvis turned on his charm and his voice soared that evening. It was a night to remember—no one there knew they were witnessing the king's final show.

As soon as Elvis returned to Graceland, he retreated into himself, preferring to be alone most of the time because he had lost all trust in "his" people. He began having nightmares: his fans had forsaken him, his money had flown with the wind, and he was left with nothing and no one. Just like he had come into the world. But at least then he had had Gladys and Vernon. Oh, yes, he still had Vernon, but his dad didn't understand him and he was sick so often himself, Elvis didn't want to burden him with his problems. And every time he passed a mirror, Elvis saw the man he had become, depressing him even further.

Elvis' spirits lifted when Lisa Marie, now nine years old, came for a visit. And it helped that he was able to talk Ginger into coming, bringing her niece, who was close to Lisa's age. He rented Libertyland, a theme park that stood on the old Memphis Fairgrounds, and they had an evening of father/daughter fun. Later that night, Elvis took some medicine for a tooth he had had filled earlier that day and then played racquetball for a while. When he tired of that, he went back into the house and sat down at his baby grand piano in the music room, his fingers quickly turning to "Blue Eyes Cryin' in the Rain."

The next morning Elvis took several packets of drugs Dr. Nick had put together for him—a cocktail of Seconal, Placidyl, Valmid, Tuinal, Demerol, and a couple of other medications. About noon, he told Ginger he was going to the bathroom, and she decided to try to get some sleep since they had been up most of the night, as usual. When she awakened an hour and a half later, she realized Elvis hadn't come to bed and went to check on him. Shocked, she found him, face down on the thick shaggy carpet in the bathroom. Her heart thumping in her chest like a hard, fast rhythm from D.J.'s drum, she called for help. Joe Esposito ran up the stairs, starting mouth-to-mouth resuscitation as soon as he saw Elvis. Soon, Vernon arrived, and seeing his son lying as still and calm as the Sea of Galilee, began to whimper, over and over, "Oh, God, son, please don't die." One wonders if Elvis were shedding tears of joy, his days of crying in the chapel forever past.

Lisa Marie, hearing all the commotion, came running, worried about her father, but Ginger gently closed the bathroom door so she couldn't see her daddy on the floor.

Dr. Nick arrived about that time, accompanied by an ambulance, and he desperately tried to revive Elvis on the quick ride to the hospital, begging him to breathe. But it was too late; Dr. Nick, nor the team of emergency room doctors who struggled with all their might to revive Elvis for more than 30 minutes, could save him.

When the word went out from the hospital that Elvis was dead, some of the Memphis media held off on announcing the news — too many rumors of Elvis' demise had circulated before. When the sad news was confirmed, radio announcer Dan Sears of WMPS was the first to broadcast what no one wanted to hear. He was followed by an announcement on WHBQ-TV, which interrupted its regularly scheduled programming to tell viewers Elvis was gone. From there, the news spread across the nation, and finally across the ocean, that the king had died — at the age of 42 — at 3:30 p.m. on August 16, 1977.

The world stood still.

Just as millions of people remember where they were when John F. Kennedy and Martin Luther King were killed, Elvis' fans have never forgotten where they were and what they were doing when they heard the news of the king's death. Doll asserts, America realized, perhaps for the first time, that the king held a place in the nation's history — for he had changed the kind of music that appealed to listeners across a generational gap. Many writers declared an era ended when Elvis died, but she disagrees. "After Elvis died, the legend evolved into a mythology, which continues to grow with each new revelation about his personal life and each new reinterpretation of his contribution to popular culture." She concludes, "Elvis the man died on August 16, 1977, but Elvis the myth continues...."

Officially, the cause of death, following an autopsy, was "cardiac arrhythmia due to an undetermined heartbeat." Fourteen drugs showed up in the blood work, and no one knows if they contributed to Elvis' death. Dr. Jerry Francisco, who performed the autopsy, had his own opinion: "He had coronary disease and mild hypertension. Butter probably produced more damage to his heart than drugs." A hospital employee revealed, "Elvis had the arteries of an eighty-year-old man...his arteries and veins were terribly corroded."

Add to that the pace at which Elvis lived — in 1973 he did 168 shows — and the stress caused by giving his all to his fans, as well as the embarrassment and regret over his failed marriage, and cardiac distress was probably inevitable. Even Lisa Marie had "a feeling," she said later, telling her father, "I don't want you to die." Elvis tried to shush her, reassuring her he wasn't going anywhere, but Lisa Marie's fears stayed with her. "He wasn't doing well. All I knew was that I had it [a feeling], and it happened." A child's intuition that became a nightmare. And she was at Graceland when it happened.

Priscilla's thoughts tossed and tumbled as she flew from her home in Los Angeles to be with her daughter. Even though they no longer lived together, the world without Elvis seemed as unimaginable as the moon falling from the sky.

Memories flooding over her, Priscilla said, "He taught me everything: how to dress, how to walk, how to apply makeup and wear my hair, how to behave, how to return love—his way. Over the years he became my father, husband, and very nearly God. Now he was gone. I felt more alone and afraid than ever in my life." She had met Elvis when she was fourteen. Now 32, she had known and loved him more than half of her life. Without him, her life suddenly seemed empty. Maybe she could feel his spirit when she arrived at Graceland.

Vernon, distraught but in control, began making plans for Elvis' funeral, which was to be held at Graceland. Elvis was laid out in a copper casket, and friends and family had a private viewing on August 17.

Tens of thousands of people—perhaps as many as 50,000, stood outside the gates of Graceland. Many of them made it inside when, after the private viewing for the family, Vernon insisted fans be allowed to walk by the casket.

Mounds of flowers covered gates, the walls, and the lawn of Graceland—a glorious garden in tribute to America's most beloved singer. In all, three thousand flower arrangements were delivered to Graceland.

The next day, in a private service for two hundred invited guests, the sounds of an organ playing "Danny Boy" wafted across the air. Ann Margret and Chet Akins, as well as Tennessee governor Ray Blanton, were present. The Colonel, oddly dressed in a blue Hawaiian shirt and a baseball cap, stood in the hall, outside the crowded living room where family, friends, and dignitaries were gathered.

As he had at Gladys' funeral, James Blackwood sang "How Great

Thou Art," one of Elvis' favorite songs, and Kathy Westmoreland, the soprano who sang with Elvis' band, also lifted her voice with "Heavenly Father." Rex Humbard talked about the time he and Elvis had prayed together, reminiscent of the chapel song's admonition that the only way to find the one true answer was to get down on your knees and pray.

Local minister C.W. Bradley talked of Elvis' "strong desire and unfailing determination," as well as acknowledging he was a "frail human being." Comedian Jackie Kahane, who had often opened Elvis' shows, delivered an impromptu eulogy, followed by several of Elvis' favorite songs, sung by Jake Hess (former lead singer for the Statesman), J.D. Sumner and the Stamps, and James Blackwood. The service concluded with more of the gospel songs Elvis had sung with such intensity — songs that had touched his soul, keeping him grounded in his faith even in the blizzard of ceaseless confusion.

After the service, crowds lined the roadway to the cemetery. Vernon had requested that Elvis be buried at Graceland, but the city had denied the necessary permits so Forest Hill Cemetery was selected for the burial site. Vernon rode in the first of seventeen white Cadillacs in the funeral cortege that had at its head a silver Cadillac and a police motorcycle escort, followed by the white hearse carrying the body of the king.

When he returned to Graceland later that day, the steel in Vernon's spine that had kept him upright and moving for the previous few days finally melted in the raging fire of his grief. He had to be helped from the car, but before he went inside the home Elvis had lovingly purchased for his parents, he issued one last request — piece by piece, flowers from all of the arrangements on the grounds should be handed to Elvis' fans who still stood outside the gates — each fan would receive a single flower to commemorate the day and the love felt for Elvis.

As for the Colonel, he went back to work as soon as the service concluded. Elvis' records would, in the end, bring in more money after his death than they did in his lifetime.

In the midst of his grief, Vernon had concerns greater than money. Someone tried to steal Elvis' body from its mausoleum in Forest Hill Cemetery (reportedly to hold it for ransom) within days after he was interred, and city officials decided it would be prudent to grant the permits they had previously denied. Vernon arranged to move both

Elvis and his mother to Graceland, placing them in the beautiful meditation garden Elvis had built as a sanctuary for prayer and contemplation. There, a large cross and statue of Christ, framed by two angels, overlooked the resting place of the two great loves of Vernon's life. Elvis was gone, but Vernon was still "taking care of business." Spirit broken, he paid final tribute to his beloved son, penning the following words for the bronze capstone for Elvis' grave:

*HE WAS A PREVIOUS GIFT FROM GOD*
*WE CHERISHED AND LOVED DEARLY*
*HE HAD A GOD-GIVEN TALENT THAT HE SHARED*
*WITH THE WORLD, AND WITHOUT A DOUBT,*
*HE BECAME THE MOST WIDELY ACCLAIMED;*
*CAPTURING THE HEARTS OF OLD AND YOUNG ALIKE*
*HE WAS ADMIRED NOT ONLY AS AN ENTERTAINER,*
*BUT AS THE GREAT HUMANITARIAN THAT HE WAS;*
*FOR HIS GENEROSITY, AND HIS KIND FEELINGS*
*FOR HIS FELLOW MAN.*
*HE REVOLUTIONALIZED THE FIELD OF MUSIC AND*
*RECEIVED ITS HIGHEST AWARDS.*
*HE BECAME A LIVING LEGEND IN HIS OWN TIME,*
*EARNING THE RESPECT AND LOVE OF MILLIONS.*
*GOD SAW THAT HE NEEDED SOME REST AND*
*CALLED HIM HOME TO BE WITH HIM.*
*WE MISS YOU, SON AND DADDY.*
*I THANK GOD HE GAVE US YOU AS OUR SON.*
*HE GAVE YOU TO US.*

~Vernon Presley

If Elvis had written his own epitaph, it might have ended with these words, "I've found the meaning of contentment. Now I'm happy with the Lord." His days of crying in the chapel were irreversibly over. And if he could have given his fans one last concert, one last word of wisdom, it might have ended with, "Take your troubles to the chapel... And your burdens will be lighter and you'll surely find the way." Elvis had found His way, and undoubtedly, he would have wanted his fans, friends, and family to find the way, joining him again someday to sing praises in the great mansion in the sky.

# 28
# REPRISAL, MY WAY

*And now, the end is here*

*And so I face the final curtain*

~Paul Anka

Elvis didn't get to state his final case in this world, but he was certain, as the song says, that he had lived a life that was full. And the record shows, he took the blows and did it his way—from flashy clothes in high school to sequined capes in Vegas; from his gyrating leg doing rock 'n' roll to his sublime delivery of "How Great Thou Art;" from hillbilly cat to king. The only place where he never did it his way was in Hollywood, where he yearned to do serious acting but never had the chance.

Elvis' fear that he wouldn't be remembered hasn't materialized. He never wrote a song and more than half of the songs he sang had been recorded by someone before him. But it is Elvis' voice that sounds in their heads when most people think of songs like "Hound Dog," "How Great Thou Art," "That's All Right, Mama," and of course, "My Way," as well as many other songs Elvis recorded.

How did a poor Southern boy travel "each and every highway," becoming a legend in his lifetime—a legend who lives on four decades after his death? The Comeback Kid of 1968 just keeps coming back into the lives of old fans and capturing the hearts of new ones. What is it about the man and his singing that continues to hold people captive?

To some, Elvis' voice, which ranged from bass to falsetto, from rough as a corncob to smooth as silk, held the key to his prowess as a singer. But others attribute his ability to captivate to the innate way he could communicate with his audiences in an uncanny fashion. Joe Esposito says, "When Elvis sings, you just feel better." Listening to his music, one not only senses what Elvis felt deep inside but also discerns that he conveyed truths, beliefs, and emotions common to all of us. Elvis sings *for* us — we can't sing as he could, so his voice becomes our voice to the world. He becomes our messenger, the outlet for our fears, our dreams, and our love. Like Elvis, many of us have a dark side, and he lets us channel our innermost thoughts through his songs. Similarly, we all have regrets, and we can thus embrace Elvis' foibles and imperfection without malice. Perhaps most importantly, we have all felt love, and for many, the passing of true love, whether by legal separation or heavenly intervention. Elvis' ballads stir our souls with longing and loss. In the list of reasons Elvis touched and held hearts, his ability to lift our spirits in gospel songs cannot be overlooked. We see ourselves in his spiritual heaviness, and his quest for grace, hope, and redemption, despite human frailty, resounds within us.

One can understand why record stores sold out of Elvis' records immediately after his death. RCA put its pressing plants on 24-hour days to try to meet demand. Within months, some of his old albums were on the charts again. RCA fed the mania, finding new ways over the years to repackage and release Elvis' songs, including some from master tapes that had never been released. One of the best results was the "Masters Series," three sets of CD's that, according to Doll, faithfully document the progression of Elvis' music from start to finish. The first set (*Elvis: The King of Rock n' Roll — The Complete '50s Masters*) follows Elvis' evolution in music from 1954 to 1958, proving, the pop culture historian asserts, that Elvis didn't pilfer, as some accuse, the style of black rhythm and blues singers and pretend he was singing his way. "Instead, the racks reveal a blending of influences and an integration of musical genres that coalesced into a commercial sound and inched closer and closer toward a universal, mainstream style."

The second set of CDs covers the 1960s and is called *Elvis: From Nashville to Memphis*. This music illustrates "that Elvis didn't entirely abandon his roots in country, gospel, and rhythm and blues after he achieved his pop style — an accusation hurled most often by rock-music critics." In spite of the "smooth, mainstream pop styling of Elvis' movie soundtracks," his blues songs, combined with his gospel pieces, show he had not forsaken his Southern heritage.

*Elvis: Walk a Mile in My Shoes* pulls together music from the 70s, showing a diversity and volume of songs that reflect all of the genres

Elvis worked with over his career. His rich baritone belts out pop songs like "It's All Right" and "Always on My Mind" and touches the soul with his impassioned delivery of songs like "Bridge Over Troubled Waters." Keogh says in such songs, Elvis retreated inside his music, losing himself in its words and sad melody. This is where we see Elvis in his purest form. Although some say his music of the 70s felt short of his earlier work, Elvis amassed an amazing collection of songs—and no one can question he still had the power to disarm his audiences. When he left the stage, he left his heart with his fans.

From his lifetime of work—and his songs that continued beyond his grave—Elvis sold more than a billion records worldwide, according to BMG (an international group of music companies involved in the management of music rights). As of 2005, his number of gold, platinum, and multi-platinum albums and singles totaled 150. Because of a change in how records are counted, the real total is around 270. No other singer in history has come close to this astounding accomplishment.

No one has to wonder why Elvis continues to be an icon in today's culture. Remarkably, this icon appeals to a diverse audience. Different people like different aspects of Elvis' songs. Country, blues, rhythm and blues, ballads, rock 'n' roll, gospel—Elvis sang something for everyone, young and old, rich and poor, black or white, urbanite or hillbilly.

Charles Kuralt, in a special CBS program aired on August 18, 1977, captured Elvis' historical significance with a humanness many newscasters missed, placing their emphasis on the parts of his life bared—perhaps with hyperbole—by the bodyguards' book that was published almost simultaneously with the king's death. Kuralt asserted, "It's hard to imagine Elvis Presley's success coming anywhere but here. He molded it out of so many American elements: country and blues and gospel and rock—a little Memphis, a little Vegas, a little arrogance, a little piety...How could we ever have felt estranged from Elvis? He was a native son."

According to the *American Demographics* magazine, 84 percent of the people in the United States say their lives have been touched by Elvis Presley in some way. An amazing 70 percent have seen an Elvis movie, 44 percent have danced to one of his songs, and 31 percent own an Elvis record, CD or video. Amazingly, 10 percent have toured Graceland and 5 percent actually saw Elvis in concert.

Even today, Elvis seems to find his way to *American Idol* most years. In 2010 he appeared live and in person (through 21st century technology) on the stage of *American Idol,* singing "If I Can Dream" in a duet with Celine Dion, kicking off Elvis Week on the show. Selecting their favorite Elvis songs, contestants chose everything from "Saved" and "Can't Help Falling in Love With You" to "Hound Dog" and "Blue Suede Shoes." In the 2011 competition, Scotty McCreery, who edged out some first-class singers to become the year's American Idol, told the audience he lived and breathed Elvis Presley from the time he could toddle around. Pictures of Scotty show him in everything from a Presley-like wig to a flamboyant outfit as a 10-year-old, lips curled in pure Elvis style. Singing "That's All Right Mama," McCreery captured kudos for his performance from all of the judges, with Randy pointing out that he showed he "isn't just a 'one trick pony,'" although some viewers disagreed, arguing that the song "was still pretty country."

The king lives on.

From a local hero who carved a place in Southern history to a defining part of generational change, Elvis made a lasting impact on youth and adults alike. Perhaps George Klein said it best: "If you're an Elvis fan, no explanation is necessary. If you're not, no explanation is possible."

Klein continues to be a solid Elvis supporter. Every day he can be heard on XM/Sirius radio, talking about Elvis and spinning his records. He sits across the street from Graceland, and ever so often he stops someone about to tour Graceland and asks them how far they traveled to get to Elvis' home. Eight hundred miles, fifteen hundred miles, three thousand miles — they come from across the United States and the world. Recently, one person who had traveled nine hundred miles confessed she has made the trip three times annually for the past six years.

What keeps fans coming to Graceland? Why do they still listen to music recorded in the last century? What made Elvis different enough to keep his hold on people over such an extended period of time? Why do fans feel so close to him they call him by his first name?

Elvis defied Tin Pan Alley, where tradition dictated mainstream pop music. With Sam Phillips' vision and Elvis' desire to be unique, he integrated the black gospel sound he had grown up around into white music, pulling from and fusing the sounds and styles of multiple genres. Whether he consciously used this approach to help move issues of race and class in the right direction, or whether it was by serendipity, Elvis opened doors when he melded blues, gospel, and pop. Sometimes disparaged for stealing his music from blacks, Elvis never failed to give credit to influences that inspired him. "The colored folks been singing it and playing it just like I'm doin' now, man, for more years than I know," Elvis told the *Charlotte Observer* in the early days of his career. He added, "They played it like that in the shanties and in their juke joints, and nobody paid it no mind 'til I goosed it up. I got it from them. Down in Tupelo, Mississippi, I used to hear old Arthur Crudup bang his box the way I do now, and I said if I ever got to the place I could feel all old Arthur felt, I'd be a music man like nobody ever saw." And that's exactly what he did.

Elvis also provided an outlet for the generational tensions of the day. Teenagers, looking for ways to express their frustration with the lifestyles of their parents and their disdain for nostalgic "grocery store" music, saw rhythm and blues, along with rock 'n' roll, as an avenue to individuality, a voice of self-expression. While other stars (the Beatles, the Rolling Stones, and others) also helped satiate their desire, Elvis started the movement with the rhythm and beat, combined with the natural sensuality, he brought to the stage. John Lennon paid tribute to Elvis' undeniable influence, saying, "Before Elvis, there was nothing."

Change was coming in America, and Elvis shaped it "his way." From teenage fashion to music, his impact shook the world. Parents accused him of leading their children to damnation, but Elvis simply sang with a heart that fueled the tastes of the new generation. As Doll notes, the image teenagers loved found its way into *Jailhouse Rock*, where Elvis played a sullen young man who projected cynicism and coolness but still showed sensitivity on the inside that was admirable. Teenager girls found him sexy and charming—his natural good looks enhanced by his curled-lip and swept-back hair made him irresistible. One young girl captured Elvis' allure: "He's just one big hunk of forbidden fruit."

In an age when kids questioned everything their parents said, teenagers may not have realized why they loved Elvis. The fact that their parents hated him was enough to make them run toward him. But more importantly, when Elvis walked off the stage, the teenagers sat exhausted, their emotions drained. The wild, impassioned beast presented a new form of expression on stage that was as different as daylight and dark. Sexy, sullen, and not afraid to sneer at those who criticized him. A perfect model for a rebellious teenager.

With the economy of the 50s giving young people discretionary money to burn, they voted for Elvis with the dollars they spent on his movies and his records. Jimmy Carter summed up what Elvis brought to the nation: "Elvis Presley was a symbol of the country's vitality, rebelliousness, and good humor."

Elvis represented rebellion—freedom from all of the constraints parents placed on their kids, escape from the traditions of the past, and a new way to express their emotions. He was part of their generation, and he created a world that at least, at the beginning, only they understood.

Sometimes Elvis' appeal to folks above the age of 20 gets lost in the controversy over his performance style, but setting aside his non-conformist image, there still remained the beautiful ballads and inspiring gospel songs that pulled in middle-aged fans. Many of them could identify not only with these genres but also with his rise to success from the depths of poverty. To some, his "rags to riches" story made him a hero, the American dream personified. Particularly in the South, where rural hardship found escape in music, Elvis' music found willing ears. Keogh notes "Elvis is not the voice of the city....In Elvis, we hear the South, the West, churchgoing folk, truck drivers with one more haul to go before daybreak. Even today, Elvis speaks for them." He is the voice of "real folks...entire families, grandmas with canes, preschoolers in party dresses...they loved him openly, the way they loved God and country."

Elvis endeared himself to people of all ages because he sang their kind of music—he had something for everyone. If they liked country, he could sing it with a twang. If they liked blues, he could swoon the words. If they liked rhythm and blues, he could thump his guitar in time with the music. If they liked ballads, he could croon a love story. And, if they liked rock 'n' roll, he could jiggle his leg and shake, rattle, and roll. And whatever he sang, he felt the words, reaching deep inside his soul for emotions that spoke both to his heart and to the hearts of his fans.

Elvis was talented, he was caring, he was generous; and, he was human. He wasn't perfect, but who on earth is? He lived at the heights and depths of life, surrounded by adoring fans and (mostly) loyal friends, yet he struggled for peace and purpose. It would be unfair and too judgmental to say his life ended in tragedy, because Elvis lives on long after his death. His gifts of music keep giving year after year, spanning generational gaps. His art form remarkably shaped the music landscape and still adds color, emotion, and dimension in the 21st century. He pioneered rockabilly and led its evolution into rock 'n' roll. He made 31 movies that spawned songs still sung today. He conquered Las Vegas (after the first time around) and toured the country to sold-out crowds in America from ocean to ocean, border to border. And from beginning to end, he asked intuitively, "For what is a man, what has he got? If not himself, then he has naught."

Elvis lived the song, "My Way," with both longing and regret. If you listen quietly, you may still hear the words whispering in the breeze outside Graceland, echoing Elvis' summation and reflection of his earthly life: "I've loved, I've laughed and cried; I've had my fill....And more, much more than this, I did it my way."

# SOURCES

Barker, Hugh and Yuval Taylor. *Faking It: The Quest for Authenticity in Popular Music*. New York: W.W. Norton and Company, 2007.

Benner, Joseph. *The Impersonal Life*. Camirallo, California: De Vorss & Co., 1917.

Bertrand, Michael T. *Race, Rock, and Elvis*. Chicago, Illinois: University of Illinois Press, 2004.

Doll, Susan. *Elvis for Dummies*. Hoboken, New Jersey: Wiley Publishing, Inc., 2009.

Dundy, Elaine. *Elvis and Gladys*. New York: Macmillan, 1985.

Edgers, Geoff. *Who Was Elvis Presley?* New York: Grosset and Dunlap, 2007.

*Elvis Presley: He Touched Me – The Gospel Music of Elvis Presley*. DVD. EMI Christian Group. Released February 15, 2005.

Esposito, Joe, with Elena Oumano. *Good Rockin' Tonight*. New York: Simon and Schuster, 1994.

Geller, Larry, and Joel Spector with Patricia Romanowski. *"If I Can Dream": Elvis' Own Story*. New York: Simon and Schuster, 1989.

Goldman, Albert. *Elvis: The Last 24 Hours*. New York: St. Martin's Paperbacks, 1991.

Guralnick, Peter. *Careless Love: The Unmaking of Elvis Presley*. New York: Little, Brown and Company, 1999.

Guralnick, Peter. *Last Train to Memphis: The Rise of Elvis Presley*. New York: Little, Brown and Company, 1994.

Guralnick, Peter. *Lost Highway: Journeys and Arrivals of American Musicians*. Boston: David R. Godine, 1979.

Guralnick, Peter, and Ernest Jorgensen. *Elvis Day by Day*. New York: Ballantine Books, 1999.

Hampton, Wilborn. *Up Close: Elvis Presley*. New York: Puffin Books, 2007.

Houk, Anita. "Maxine." *Commercial Appeal Mid-South Magazine*, December 2, 1984.

Hoppe, Sherry L., and Bruce W. Speck. *Maxine Smith's Unwilling Pupils: Lessons Learned in Memphis' Civil Rights Classroom*. Knoxville, Tennessee: University of Tennessee Press, 2007.

Keogh, Pamela Clarke. *Elvis Presley: The Man. The Life. The Legend*. New

York: Simon and Schuster, 2004.

McKeon, Elizabeth and Linda Everett (eds.). *Elvis Speaks: Thoughts on Fame, Family, Music and More in His Own Words*. Nashville, Tennessee: Cumberland House Publishing, 2004.

Marsh, Dave. *Elvis*. New York: Times Books, 1982.

Mason, Bobbie Ann. *Elvis Presley*. New York: Viking Press, 2002.

Moore, Scotty, as told to James Dickerson. *That's Alright, Elvis: The Untold Story of Elvis's First Guitarist and Manager, Scotty Moore*. New York: Schirmer, 1997.

NWS office http://tennesseewx.com/index.php?topic=2466.0 (Accessed March 9, 2011).

Presley, Priscilla Beaulieu, with Sandra Harmon. *Elvis and Me*. New York: G.P. Putnam's Sons, 1985.

*TV Radio Mirror*, cited in Guralnick, Peter. *Last Train to Memphis: The Rise of Elvis Presley*. New York: Little, Brown and Company, 1994.

Tucker, Stephen. "Rethinking Elvis and the Rockabilly Moment." In *In Search of Elvis: Music, Race, Art, Religion*, edited by Vernon Chadwick. Boulder, Colorado: Westview Press, 1997.

Williams, Bill. Cited in Barker, Hugh and Yuval Taylor. *Faking It. The Quest for Authenticity in Popular Music*. New York: W.W. Norton & Co., 2007.

## COPYRIGHT PERMISSIONS

# ACKNOWLEDGMENTS

When Carol Daniels, the publisher of Wakestone Press, approached me about writing one of the first books in Wakestone's Legacy Series, she presented 10 or so famous people for my consideration. When I saw Elvis Presley's name on the list, I was intrigued but wondered what I could possibly add to the myriad books on the legendary king of rock 'n' roll. Because I was working on a book about addiction at the time, I decided that I might bring perspective on that aspect of his life. When I began my research, though, I immediately realized there was so much more to be discovered and presented — although a number of writers have explored why Elvis electrified audiences and continues to captivate listeners, the best books were usually long and overly detailed. My goal thus became to examine what made Elvis appealing to so many people in a fairly short yet comprehensive book. The result, *My Way*, is offered as a tribute to a man whose human frailties don't diminish his legacy of music.

Having grown up loving Elvis' songs, through writing this book I found not only a new and deeper appreciation for his evolution as an entertainer but also a keen sense of his search for spirituality and purpose. I am grateful to Carol for the opportunity to write this book. I also appreciate Frank Daniels, whose editing skills are invaluable. Special thanks go to Nanette Noffsinger and Amy Jaramillo of Burke Hollow Media for their expertise and dedication to publicizing my books.

In researching material for *My Way*, I found Peter Guralnick's two-volume biography (*Last Train to Memphis* and *Careless Love*) to be the most definitive Elvis biography available. I highly recommend Guralnick's work for its remarkable detail and am deeply indebted to this valuable resource. Two other sources deserve particular mention: Pamela Clarke Keogh's book, *Elvis Presley — The Man, the Life, the Legend*, provided an exceptionally perceptive view of many aspects of the king's life; and, Susan Doll's *Elvis for Dummies* was of singular assistance in examining and evaluating Elvis' music and movies in terms of iconography and lasting significance.

# Sherry Lee Hoppe

Sherry Hoppe is the author of *A Matter of Conscience, Redemption of a hometown hero, Bobby Hoppe; Sips of Sustenance: Grieving the Loss of Your Spouse;* and *Faces of Grief: Stories of Surviving Sorrow and Finding Hope;* as well as authoring and editing books on higher education for the academic market, including two books on spirituality, and a history of a prominent civil rights leader from Memphis, Tennessee. Dr. Hoppe's first career was as a counselor before getting her Ed.D. in higher education and entering the post-secondary academic world. She is president emeritus of Austin Peay State University and served as president at Roane State College and Nashville State College.

Other Wakestone Press books by Sherry L. Hoppe

**A Matter of Conscience**, *Redemption of a hometown hero, Bobby Hoppe.* With Dennie B. Burke.
ISBN: 978-1-60956-001-0

**Sips of Sustenance**, Grieving the Loss of Your Spouse.
ISBN: 978-1-60956-007-2

**Faces of Grief**, Stories of Surviving Sorrow and Finding Hope.
ISBN: 978-1-60956-010-2